W9-CXU-804

DATE DUE

Gunhild Jørgensen

The Techniques of China Painting

VAN NOSTRAND REINHOLD COMPANY
New York Cincinnati Toronto London Melbourne

Van Nostrand Reinhold Company Regional Offices:
New York Cincinnati Chicago Millbrae Dallas

Van Nostrand Company International Offices:
London Toronto Melbourne

This title was originally published in Danish
under the title of Porcelænsmaling strøg for strøg
by Høst & Søns Forlag, Copenhagen, Denmark.

Copyright © for Porcelænsmaling strøg for strøg
Høst & Søns Forlag, Copenhagen, Denmark, 1971.
English translation copyright ©
Van Nostrand Reinhold Company Ltd., 1974

Library of Congress Catalog Card Number: 73-3941
ISBN: 0 442 29989 3

Translated from the Danish by Hugh Young

This book is set in Garamond and is filmset and printed by
BAS Printers Limited, Wallop, Hampshire

Published by Van Nostrand Reinhold Company,
450 West 33rd Street, New York, N.Y. 10001 and
Van Nostrand Reinhold Company Ltd.,
25–28 Buckingham Gate, London S.W.1E 6LQ

16 15 14 13 12 11 10 9 8 7 6 5 4 3 2 1

Library of Congress Cataloging in Publication Data
Jørgensen, Gunhild 1919 –
The techniques of China painting.
Translation of Porcelænsmaling strøg for strøg.
1. China painting. 1. Title.
NK4605. J613   738.1'5   73-3941
ISBN 0-442-29989-3

Contents

Foreword

This book is a primer for china painting, and is intended for private study and as a background to class instruction.

The material and arrangement of the book is based on many years' teaching experience, including academic and technical experiments, together with the help of other teachers who have given me the benefit of their experience. I have tried to arrange the lessons in such a way that there is a logical progression, so that china painters may proceed step-by-step.

This is not therefore primarily a pattern book. Except for the models in the colour section the only others are the illustrations required for an understanding of the text. The main aim has been to provide a comprehensive text on all aspects of china painting, including the technical skills involved, how to construct patterns, composition and lessons on colour harmony.

I hope though that readers will also find material to stimulate their imagination. There are enough ideas here for both the beginner and the experienced painter to encourage development of a free and personal style.

Gunhild Jørgensen

Warning

It has become known that certain china paints may release lead and other metallic compounds when attacked by acids that are present in or are used in connection with certain foodstuffs, notably vinegar and fruit juices.

Metal release can pose difficult problems as the factors governing it are many and varied. Although a balanced glaze will be of some help it may not provide the whole answer. This is because the amount of lead released by a glaze need not necessarily be proportional to the amount of lead contained in it. A 'safe' glaze may be made 'unsafe' by minor modifications and changes, for example in the kiln temperature or the presence of lead vapours in the kiln from previous firings.

In both America and the United Kingdom specifications have been published indicating permissible limits. All catalogues of ceramic suppliers now print warning notices about the risks involved and detailed instructions. Many firms who retail large quantities to schools and other educational institutions leave out colours which carry definite risks.

Several firms run testing services in their laboratories for fired wares to see if they fall within the specified limits. A scale of fees is charged.

A Note on the Colours Used in this Book

The descriptions of the fifteen colours (e.g. dark yellow, light blue, etc.) used in this book are not precise. The many suppliers of on-glaze paints describe what are similar colours with different names. Moreover, it is rare that any one supplier will be able to reproduce the same shade for any one colour.

However, to give the reader an idea of what is meant by the descriptions in this book, the colours are reproduced on p. 49. It will help you to match these colours with those that you have already, or intend to buy.

Part One

1. On Decoration

The origin of the art of decoration is lost in the prehistory of man, and it is safe to say that the urge to decorate lies deep in human nature. From the beginning of time men have both decorated their own bodies with painted and scratched lines and patterns and painted their everyday articles with ornaments and pictures. The urge to decorate is the same the world over.

We can read in books on cultural history, ethnography and the history of art about the ornaments and the picture writing that man has used through the centuries, and we can see the objects themselves in museums throughout the world.

Many of the ornaments and the detailed decorations with which men have brightened their daily lives are timeless. There are patterns and ornaments that speak to us plainly through the language of their form. Motifs were often created when man was making implements and tools for his own use.

Other things belong more firmly in their own period. They had to follow a prevailing taste or fashion among certain classes and *milieus*, and were intended for sale and not for the maker's personal use. It will often be harder to appreciate such things without some knowledge of the background of the period and of those who bought them.

The period and the society to which a decorated object belongs, the materials used and the technical ability displayed, make their mark both in the design of the object and in the way in which it was used.

Each cultural era and each stage of development is foreshadowed in the period or periods that came before and in the development of society. The more you look at the designs and the conditions that lie behind us, the better you can understand yourself, your own situation and your own period. You do not have to be an artist

Straight-sided clay beakers found in Stone Age excavations in Jutland. The beakers date from about 1900 BC. The decoration is built up symmetrically from patterns of lines. This is a style on which there have been infinite variations through the ages, one that will always be equally useful whether you use the lines as a starting-point to create a design or employ them as decorations by themselves. The beakers are now in the National Museum in Copenhagen.

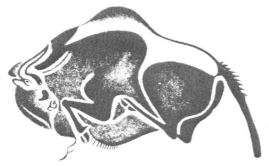

The aurochs is a reproduction of an Ice Age painting found on a rock wall in the Altamira caves in Spain. A few masterly strokes have made the plunging ox natural and life-like. Here is something that anyone who paints animals can learn from.

or art historian to understand such things; you only have to be interested in them.

In the most ancient cultures art was often tied up with magic. It took on a religious significance in relation to all that surrounded man and his struggle to come to terms with his existence, with his fear of the unknown and with his desire for success in the hunt for food. Some experts believe that the famous cave paintings in southern France and northern Spain were painted for some magic purpose and then when a man drew a picture of what he wanted, he almost had it in his power.

In the Muslim countries we see how all decoration has developed into stylized, geometric motifs, since the Koran forbids the depiction of human beings.

Today the magic has turned into symbols. Everyone knows the heart, the cross and the anchor twined together, for instance on a brooch, as a symbol of faith, hope and charity – and the symbolic orange-blossom in a bride's hair or bouquet.

The Skarpsalling bowl, a clay bowl from Danish pre-history (later Stone Age).

The bowl, reckoned to be one of the most beautiful pre-historic finds in the North, was named after the district of Skarpsalling in North Jutland, where it was found. It is now in the National Museum, Copenhagen.

The things that people made in the old days were functional – that is, they were designed to serve some specific purpose. Sometimes they struck a happy medium so that what decoration there was served a purpose. One outstanding example is the Skarpsalling pot – a clay pot from early Danish times, on which there are grooves that make the lugs or ears easier to hold. If you study the Skarpsalling pot more closely, you can learn something important about decoration. The individual parts of the pattern all harmonize with the material and with its structure, and they follow the form of the pot exactly. Decoration and form thus make a unity.

The decoration, scratched in the wet clay, was hardly painted at all, and so differs from what we are concerned with in the field of china painting. None the less the need for harmony between form and decoration was the same then as it is now.

We live in a technological age, in which many people have lost interest in what is made by hand and the natural creativity that stems from it. Creativity has not been allowed to develop because there has been no use for our creation. Not until things are pointed out to us do we appreciate what has been created, or perhaps we suddenly become perceptive when we look at something simple and see the beauty in a piece of craftwork, where everything superfluous has been eliminated and materials, form and colour are bound together in the simplest possible alliance.

We are surrounded by pictures and colours every day, from the garish posters and advertisements that urge us to buy or consume this or that product, to the illustrations in books, magazines and newspapers and the images on television. We have so many images and patterns all round us that we run the risk of being blinded.

When the attacks on our vision become altogether too disturbing and confusing we can easily get to the point where we see without really noticing. Everything slips past us and we don't take in the half of it. If we lose the capacity to see, we lose at the same time the capacity for surprise and delight. We lose a part of ourselves.

Bowl sculpture by Nell Bernard, an example of what a present-day sculptor produces when inspired by the Skarpsalling bowl.

In place of the clay bowl we now have a ceramic sculpture, one half of which grows up into a new abstract figure, on to which the line ornamentation spills over. An inspiration from long ago that lives on today.

A present-day work of art – a game with lines – you can't scratch patterns out on china as you can on the soft, unfired clay, but you can still make use of linear designs and ornaments when you use a technique suitable for painting on china. The line decoration on this bowl is done with a fine brush and china paints.

7

This happens unconsciously, so that we ourselves don't notice it. When we create, we have an opportunity to rediscover some of our lost capacities. Our urge to be creative can take many forms. For many, the way lies through an enjoyment of painting china. This book is for them.

Its aim is to allow the reader to achieve the spontaneity and the joy in creation that have been a part of the human condition through the ages. You can achieve this by taking a brush in your hand, playing freely with the working materials of the artist and finally creating something which never existed before and which is a personal expression of yourself – and which may well give pleasure to others.

Under-glaze painting – the 'Muselmalet' set at the Royal Danish Porcelain Factory.

2. On China Painting and Drawing

China Painting

There are two kinds of china painting: under-glaze painting and on-glaze painting. Under-glaze painting is used chiefly by manufacturers of porcelain. The painting is done on the porous, raw surface of the china before it is glazed and fired in the kiln.

It is a very lengthy process and not really suitable for amateurs, unless you want to go in for glazing and firing yourself, in which case you will have to acquire your own kiln.

On-glaze painting is painting on the ready-glazed white china which is then fired after painting. This is the type of china painting described and discussed in this book.

China painting is a game involving colours and shapes, and as you go through the book I hope you will acquire a feeling for how colours can be made to harmonize. Not everybody has a natural feeling for colour, any more than an ear for music. This book tells you, section by section, some of the rules you can go by if you feel unsure; it represents, as it were, a 'score' to refer to.

To give you a feeling for colours and their use, you are advised in the first section of the book to get the three primary colours, yellow, red and blue. These three colours will form a basis for further work and make it easier for you to make progress.

Primary colours are colours that can't be made by mixing other colours. You can on the other hand mix the primary colours together to make other colours, and in so doing you get a starting-point for building up a colour chart which opens up new possibilities for working in colour, not only in china painting but in any field in which you may have to put colours together.

On-glaze painting. The decorations on both vases are done without models, by using sketches which are first tried out on paper.

    The starting-point for the pattern on the left-hand vase was a drawing in fibre-pen on squared paper of various kinds of lines, which were then combined. The chosen pattern was drawn in the size that naturally fitted the vase.

    The basis of the pattern on the vase on the right was a number of lightning sketches of imaginary flowers with the starting-point in circles, using a soft pencil on sketching paper. The best 'blooms' were selected and adapted to the form of the vase.

Colour Charts

There are various ways of working out colour charts. The drawing shows one that has been arranged as a 'colour compass'. Compasses of this kind, which make suggestions for choice of colours, are used in connection with most of the illustrations in this book.

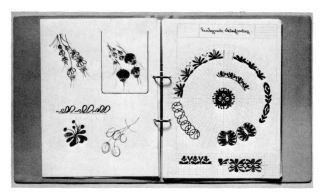

Loose-leaf working binder. As soon as you have completed the exercises on the first strokes you will find a working binder useful. It is invaluable both for sketching and for recording events occurring during your work.

On the compass, the primary colours – the strong-hued colours yellow, red and blue – are marked with arrows pointing to the letters Y(ellow), R(ed) and B(lue). The colours are marked with dots round the circle in such a way that there is the same distance between each pair of colours. The little lines on the circle mean that the primary colours can be mixed so as to make the so-called 'secondary' colours: red and yellow = O(range), blue and red = V(iolet – actually a brownish violet) and blue and yellow = Gr(een).

You can arrange the strong-hued colours in a circle, and when you do so each colour will lie next to the colour nearest to it in hue. (By hue we understand that property which determines whether we call something, for example, yellow or orange, red, violet, blue, green and so on.) See the colour chart on p. 49.

A mixture of blue and red always gives a brownish violet, as pointed out above; so as you buy more colours it will be best to get the exact shade of violet you want.

If you mix in the proportion of one part of yellow, two of red and three of blue, the three primary colours, you get what is virtually black, and this is put in the middle of the compass as a 'pole'. The primary colours and the three secondary colours are together known as the main colours.

Grey and black – the neutral or 'colourless' colour – are included in the illustrations but cannot be marked on the colour compass. The grey colour scale, as it is called, which comprises the blacks and greys, is discussed in more detail on p. 24.

Drawing on China and Paper
To avoid too much dependence on a preliminary drawing copied on to the china, we shall work from the start quite freely with the brush-strokes, and the only drawings will be a few sketched guide-lines. These guide-lines are so simple that they can be drawn straight on to the china with a pencil, without being sketched on paper first. If a china surface is dampened with alcohol and then allowed to dry you can draw on it with an ordinary pencil; the pencil lines will disappear during firing. When you work with more complicated patterns, it will be a good idea – at first, anyway – to do a preparatory sketch on paper. In this case it is useful to have a loose-leaf block.

For the first rough sketches you may find it best to use a fibre pen – and A4 typing paper. The fibre pen is a rough tool for drawing and has the advantage of eliminating unnecessary attention to detail, and therefore you can simplify your designs. The overall effect and coherence is more important than the details.

Whether or not you want to use the same instrument for making the fair copy of your drawing must depend on what kind of design it is. If it is a detailed motif, you will in most cases want to make the copy with an ordinary pencil. You may want to use squared paper or circle-paper for the fair copy, according to how the model is to be used. That will also help you in placing the motif on the china object. For enlarging or reducing motifs, see p. 103.

A loose leaf from the binder, showing some of the very first stages by which a design is arrived at.

The motif has been fair-copied to fit the vase, this time in pencil – and then painted on with watercolour.

Using the selected sketch or drawing as a pattern, you can draw the guide-lines, and if necessary the model itself, on the china, using a pencil as described above. You can also use a china pencil, with which you can draw straight on to the china without preparation. China pencils should be used with care, however: they make a very strong mark which can make the china paints dirty and thus make you lose control over the tone. It is best, therefore, to use them only to mark guide-points for the placing of the decoration. The marks of such a pencil can be cleaned off the china with water. However, if you use a china pencil for sketching on paper, remember that the line cannot be rubbed out.

Of course you can also paint straight on to the china, with or without a preliminary drawing, if you are quite sure that you know what you want, have an absolutely clear idea about the shape and the colour of your motif,

Vase with a fancy branch. The decoration has been developed from a lightning sketch done in the working binder with fibre-pen.

Right. Painting straight on to the china.

and about the right position to place it. Most people will need a lot of practice and experience before they can do that successfully.

Before you begin to draw or paint you should take a little time to relax completely so that you are not in any way tense. Lean well back in your chair and let your arms hang down by your sides. This should make you hold your brush or pencil more loosely, more freely and more lightly. If while you are working you find your muscles tightening up so that your hand gets tense, take a moment off to relax. The work will go much more easily afterwards.

Guide-lines for Placing the Design on the China

You can draw these with pencil and ruler, but as additional help in transferring the lines you can use squared paper (for rectangular objects) or circle-paper (for round objects).

Place the object on the paper and draw its outline; then on the outline mark off the required divisions. For objects that stand up, hold the ruler up along the side of the object from the points marked on the paper. If you need marks both at the top and at the bottom of the object, transfer the marks from the paper to the china before drawing the lines.

If the object is curved, like that shown here, the guide-lines can be drawn with the help of a curved ruler.

If you have a banding-wheel (which you don't actually need as a beginner), you can trace the guide-lines quickly and safely. If the lines are to be traced round a bowl, as shown here, you need only mark off the distances on one of the vertical axes, and lines can be put on wherever you want them.

If you are doing the job by hand, it can be difficult to trace the lines, for instance in the middle of a bowl. You can do it on the side by holding the pencil with thumb and forefinger and supporting your hand against the side of the object with your middle finger.

If you use a banding-wheel, be sure to place the object exactly over the centre. This applies not only to a bowl such as is shown here, but also to flat things, where besides radii you also need to divide the circle. It can be quite hard to get the object exactly in the centre. The picture shows how you can use a piece of circle-paper, clipped on. The circle-paper is stuck to the wheel with tape and the objects can then be quickly fitted into the circle which corresponds with it.

Using a piece of circle-paper.

Everyone who paints china should make it one of their aims to reach the stage at which they can create their own personally designed decorations. With only a handful of the materials used by beginners you can make trial efforts in this direction, starting from any one of the exercises in this book.

3. Basic Materials and Equipment

Materials

  yellow, red and blue china paints and paint-tubes
  1 brush + handle and 10mm. ($\frac{1}{3}$in.) of valve rubber
  1 bottle copaiba balsam or other oil
  1 bottle vegetable turpentine
  1 turpentine cup
  1 knife-shaped spatula
  1 fine drawing pen
  2 white tiles

Apart from the tiles you can buy all these materials at any artists' suppliers. See also the note on tiles on p. 20.

Other Aids

It is a good idea to work on a light underlay of thin white card. The card can be used for making notes while you work without having to leave the table.

To clean and dry the china, use a fluff-free cloth and a little alcohol.

The list of materials does not include a palette. As a beginner you can manage very well with a tile on which to mix your colours. Various kinds of palette can of course be bought from artists' suppliers, including some with lids.

It is also useful to have a tape-measure or a ruler handy.

China Paints

You can buy china paints at oils' suppliers in packets containing 5 grams. You can get about a hundred different colours. One set of colours, the purple colours – a description that includes the violet paints – contains gold, and so they are a bit more expensive than other paints. They are therefore sold also in packets of only $2\frac{1}{2}$ grams.

The actual material of the paint, the 'pigment', is produced by the chemical combination of different elements that give the appropriate colour to the paint. The pigments have different densities, so that 5 grams in weight does not make the same amount of every colour.

When you paint, you must be careful to note that china paints do not take on their true colour – the pure colour – until they are 'fired' and fixed in the china. The violets, which contain gold, change most of all in firing. In powder form they are a grey-violet, and only become what we think of as violet after the final firing.

Not all pigments can be used together in the same mixture, and there are some colours that need to be fired at a different temperature from that which is normal for china paints.

Before you start painting you will do well to get a box in which to store your equipment and materials. Paint-boxes with spaces specially laid out for the purpose can be bought in all art shops.

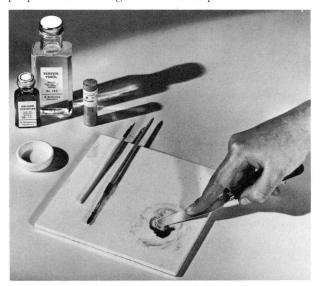

Grinding the paint is an important part of work with china paints. Press down on the blade of the spatula with your index finger and move it round and round with a circular motion.

4. How the Materials are Used

For the first practice strokes, use the following mixture:

powder paint	red, about 4mm.
oil	fat oil; add about half as much fat oil as powder
turpentine	add a few drops to the powder; turpentine is constantly added during painting, since it dries off

Grinding the Paint

One of the tiles listed with the materials is intended to be used as a palette when you are mixing the paints; the other is to paint your practice strokes on. Clean grease and dirt off the tiles with alcohol and lay them on the white card underlay. Next mix the paint with oil and turpentine on the palette, at the same time crushing the small grains that the powder paint consists of. This is called 'grinding' the paint.

When you first start painting you must make a note of how far the paint goes, so that you can get an idea of how much to prepare on the palette for a given motif.

Powder Paint

We have measured the powder paint here in millimetres. This may seem a rather unusual way of measuring weight, but it works very well. When we are told to use '4mm.' of paint for a practice stroke, that means enough paint to cover 4mm. of the point of the spatula; and since you use the spatula to take the paint out of the tube, you have an immediate visual measure. You are not meant to measure it with a ruler; you just estimate it by eye.

For the first practice strokes, use red paint but make sure that it can be mixed with other paints, as not all red pigments are miscible.

Start with the red though, as it is easier to grind and more supple to work with than, for instance, blue paints.

Oil – the Binding Agent

The function of the oil is to bind the paint to the china, and it also helps to make the paint more supple.

Take the oil directly from the bottle by dipping the plastic handle of a fine drawing pen into it and dripping it beside the heap of powder paint. (Shut the bottle after use to keep out dust and prevent drying.) Lay the handle used for dripping on the palette so that it is handy if you need to use more oil. (The fine drawing pen is included in the list of materials on p. 13, but you won't use the pen itself until later.)

Taking the oil out of a bottle.

The amount of oil that has to be added is something you gradually get an instinct for. It can be laid down as a firm rule that you should always add at least half the volume of oil as there is powder paint. Some pigments need more oil than others, and it is generally true to say that dark blue and violet paints need more oil than the others. Avoid going to the opposite extreme, however, and adding too much: paint that contains too much oil will 'boil up' in the firing or scale off.

Add oil to the paint only once, at the start, except for the few drops you may have to add later to keep the paint at the right consistency for painting.

Turpentine – the Softener

Turpentine is kept in a colour bowl so that the bottom is well covered. The bottle is always kept shut to prevent drying. A few drops are added to the paint on the palette, taken from the colour bowl with the spatula.

The turpentine breaks down the paint and makes it soft enough to paint with. It won't spoil the paint if you get too much turpentine in it, because, as mentioned before, turpentine dries very quickly.

If you want to, you can speed up the drying by breathing on the paint as you grind it. The longer you grind the paint the more supple it becomes, so add too much turpentine rather than too little.

As the turpentine in the colour bowl gradually dries it leaves a residue in the form of a sticky yellow oil. This oil – fat oil, as it is called – can be used for mixing china paints instead of copaiba balsam, but it is better to buy it from your supplier. You use it in the same way and in the same quantities as copaiba balsam.

We have preferred copaiba balsam in this book because it is more supple, and you can both paint with it and use it for what is called laying a ground – as we shall see later.

Brushes

Brushes for china painting can be bought in many sizes and qualities and include both pen-bag brushes (which are most commonly used) and brushes fitted with handles. In the first type the hairs are fitted to a little holder made from a quill. The hollow quill is fitted to a wooden handle. (See the following section.)

The type and size of brushes are denoted by series numbers and size numbers. The series number tells you something about the quality of the brush and what kind of hairs it has. The size number tells you the size of the brush in its particular series: the lower the number, the shorter and thinner the brush.

To the beginner and the advanced painter alike, a general decoration brush is specially useful, partly because it is of good quality, and partly because, thanks to the thickness and length of its hairs, it can be used for most purposes in china painting.

Other types of brush will be described as we go along.

A general decoration Brush.

Testing Paints

If you use loose brushes, you fit them to the handle before use. This is done as follows: roll a little piece of valve rubber 6–10mm. ($\frac{1}{4}$–$\frac{1}{3}$in.) on to the handle and then put the brush on so that it holds fast to the rubber. This will prevent the quill that holds the hairs of the brush from buckling.

A new brush is generally stiff and should be softened with turpentine before use; but don't let it stand in the turpentine or the hairs will be bent and the brush spoiled. Also, too much turpentine will in time dissolve the rubber; if that happens fit a new piece.

When you are ready to start painting, dip the tip of the brush in turpentine and press it out on the side of the turpentine cup; then draw the brush once or twice lightly through the paint and test, with a stroke on the palette, whether the consistency of the mixed paint is right. The strokes should look clean and clear with a certain transparency from the china in the thin tones, and the paint should hold its shape at the outer sides of the strokes without running.

If the brush won't 'glide', it may be because there is too little oil or turpentine in the paint. Look out for the following:

(1) If the paint quickly goes matt, add a little more oil. Too little oil in the paint will result in its not sinking deeply enough in the glaze of the china when it is fired, so that the painted motif will wear off. Also, if you don't use enough oil, the paint will look matt and dull after firing.

(2) If the paint looks transparent and very shiny and liquid, you have used too much oil. You can add a little dry powder, but then you must grind it again so that the new paint is crushed.

(3) If the paint is too sticky but contains enough oil, add a few drops of turpentine and grind the paint again so that it becomes properly supple.

5. Painting the First Strokes

A matchbox decorated with designs developed from the first practice strokes. Small tiles can also be used for other purposes; for example, you can fit them with chains and hang them up as ornaments.

On the tile to the extreme right there is a colour motif which corresponds to the colour circle printed on page 49. The strokes are added one by one each time you work with a new colour, and as you progress you can go on to the intermediate colours, either mixing them yourself or buying them ready-mixed. By progressing in this way you will obtain an understanding of work with colours. When, as in this case, you have worked with all the main colours, it is wise to have the tile fired before adding new strokes.

It is a good idea both for beginners and for advanced painters to practise a few strokes so as to get the feeling both of the use of the brush and of the effect of the paint before actually painting the motif. As a beginner in china painting you will be wise to confine yourself to painting on flat objects, which are much easier to work with than three-dimensional shapes.

The practice strokes that follow are intended for painting on a tile as a first exercise, from which you can go on as you learn to alter the breadth and length of the strokes in different ways by changing the pressure and by varied use of the brush.

No matter how the brush is used, the paint should be put on very thinly and look as if it has been 'breathed' on to the surface.

Ordinary Strokes

Charge the brush as described in the section on testing paints (p. 15). Lay half the surface of the brush against the tile and draw it downwards (towards you), lifting the brush gently off the surface so that the stroke gets narrower until the brush is finally taken off the tile altogether.

Ordinary strokes

Narrow and Pointed Strokes

You make this kind of stroke by putting the tip of the brush on to the surface and drawing it downwards with light pressure, at the same time lifting the brush so that the stroke narrows as described above.

Narrow and pointed strokes

Broad Strokes

You get a broad stroke by laying a large part of the surface of the brush against the china and drawing it downwards, then taking it off quite suddenly.

Broad strokes

You will probably find it useful to practise the strokes over and over again, until there is no more room on the tile. You can then clean the tile with a cloth, dampened with a little turpentine; or if the paint is still fresh and has not dried in you can use spirit. As you gradually master the strokes you can paint them on a new tile, either freehand straight on to the surface or on lines sketched with a pencil. See p. 10 for directions about preliminary pencil sketches.

Combination of strokes

When the tile is completely covered it can be fired, and then you will have a painted survey of all the different strokes. You may also find these helpful when you come to put the strokes together.

As soon as you are fairly confident about executing just a few of the strokes, you can start putting them together to make decorations.

Bonbonnière – *three examples* (*above*)
Lampstand (*left*)
Looking-glass (*below*)

6. Putting the Strokes Together on Square Surfaces

The diagram below shows how the individual strokes can be combined to form decorations with the help of lines. For this you should use square tiles about 2in. square. (See p. 20.)

As the first aid to a harmonious combination of strokes use very simple dividing lines – vertical and horizontal centre-lines and diagonals from corner to corner. To get varied design effects, guide-lines can be drawn round the outside in the form of circles or curves. This has been done here in an easy and simple way by the use of different sized coins laid either in the middle of the tile or off-centre. With practice, you will only need to draw part of the circles. If you have bought a stencil, that can be used in a similar way.

Draw the guide-lines on a tile cleaned with spirit, using a ruler and an ordinary pencil. The illustration shows how different sizes of strokes can be drawn freehand if you use the guide-lines to place them correctly.

As the colour compasses above show, each of the patterns is drawn in one of the strong colours (i.e. the primary colours and the secondary colours obtained by mixing them).

If you want to combine the strokes with lines you can use some of the guide-lines as part of the pattern. In that case you must paint in the lines in colour, or else they will disappear in the firing.

The thin lines and dots shown below are drawn with the tip of the brush. Use a dark colour to give character to the pattern. If you don't have a dark colour, you can get a close approximation of black by mixing all three primary colours together. For this purpose you can use the paint left over from the other exercises. Dried paint can be used again if you grind it with turpentine.

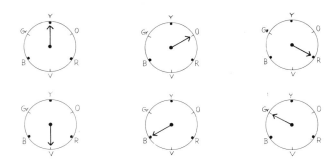

Six colour compasses – primary and intermediate colours, one for each square in the diagram below.

Sketches suggested for square tiles. The first three motifs are each painted in one of the primary colours. The last three are painted in the intermediate colours orange, violet and green, which are made by mixing the three primary colours in pairs. You can use either newly ground paints or powder paints. Of course you can also buy ready-mixed colours, and they have a rather brighter tone than those you mix yourself.

The tone for each motif is varied from light to dark. This effect can be achieved by putting on the paint in varying degrees of thickness. If you want a darker tone you can add a small amount of black paint to the relevant colour.

Thin lines and dots can be painted with an ordinary brush, making the hair come to a point by rolling it lightly as you draw it through the paint. You can use lines and dots to make decorations by themselves, as in this picture.

The tiles used here are waterproof and frostproof; they have a slightly uneven surface, so that they need a rather coarser style of decoration than china. The motif here is painted with the biggest stroke you can manage with a china painting brush.

After firing the tile is glued to a piece of ready-cut chipboard with contact-glue. This tile can be used as a table-mat.

You can vary your patterns by changing the position of the guide-lines on the tile. Try different combinations of circles and curves, for instance. Afterwards you can put the strokes you have practised either on or above the guide-lines. Either partly or completely filling in the spaces between the lines also opens up new possibilities.

Whether you paint the guide-lines in with colour so that they form an element in the completed pattern, or just draw them in with pencil so that they disappear with firing, you will find that they help you to create a variety of designs from the very beginning.

Tiles

As a beginner at china painting you can paint on the ordinary white wall-tiles used in the building industry. Suitable makes at a cheap price are Rako and Brilliant. But these wall-tiles are not really a very good medium for china painting because of their soft texture – that is, both the body of the tiles and the glaze are soft. They get worn more quickly if you use them, for instance, as a teapot stand than they do when used to build a wall in a bathroom, and when used as loose tiles they easily crack.

Even if you begin by using cheap tiles, as soon as you have had practice and experience in brushwork you should get tiles of a good quality, even though they will be a little dearer.

You can get a considerable choice of tiles in all big stores that sell building materials. You can also get the tiles used for laying floors; several makes of this kind of tile are quite suitable for painting on with china paints.

The slightly more expensive white 'Supramosflise' tiles can be recommended, obtainable in the size 150 mm. × 150 mm. × 12·5 mm. (6in. × 6in. × $\frac{1}{2}$in.). This tile is resistant to water and frost and so can be used both indoors and out.

The small white tiles, 50 mm. (2in.) square, are obtainable under the name of Mettlach tiles. Besides white you can get them in a number of pastel shades, but these are not always as suitable for china painting as white. Paints change their character when painted on a coloured ground. However, you can get some special effects by using the colour of the tiles. That is true also of the waterproof and frostproof tiles, whose glaze is sprayed on so that they have a slightly uneven surface. If you use a slightly course style of decoration on it, you will find it outstandingly well suited for china painting. Two sizes are obtainable, 96 × 96 × 7mm. and 196 × 196 × 10mm. (3.8 × 3.8 × 0.3in. and 7.8 × 7.8 × 0.4in.).

Coarser tiles than those mentioned here, both glazed and unglazed, have recently won acceptance among china painters. They require a coarser style of painting and consequently larger brushes than those used in this book. (See p. 111 for suppliers of tiles.)

If you prefer to paint on real china instead of tiles from the very beginning, read the section on china on p. 28.

A combination of strokes – six examples.

7. Painting Curved Strokes

When you have been through the first strokes and painted one or two little things, you ought to know enough about the use of the materials and to have had enough practice to begin to paint curved strokes and combine them with straight strokes.

On the teapot, the motif subject goes back to the tile; one little stroke more is added in the middle and then the subject is complimented by its mirror image.

Symmetrical patterns like this can be tried out in advance by drawing the motif with a fibre-pen on transparent paper. Then fold the paper along the centre-line of the pattern and trace the pattern from the under-side of the paper.

When the paper is unfolded you will have the complete symmetrical pattern; try adding more details as desired.

Some examples of curved strokes.

The diagram on p. 23 shows how curved strokes can become decorative ornamental strokes when you vary their size and their composition. The strokes are painted here freehand, without any kind of guide-lines. When the designs are to be placed on the china, you must naturally give some thought first to the form and placing of the ornaments.

The cock was the result of an absolutely free play with a combination of strokes inside a circle, using two colours. Use your imagination to make other animal shapes in this way.

This tile decoration is made up by repeating one motif subject of five strokes. The guide-lines for the extension of the pattern are drawn with the help of squared paper.

This decoration can be regarded as a practice for the next two illustrations.

The brush movement is much the same as we have worked with before, so far as pressure is concerned. The characteristic pressure that gives variety to the stroke and brings it to life is called 'accentuation'. You now paint the strokes with a curved movement to the left or right, while the straight strokes are painted by drawing the brush straight down towards you. You can develop this technique to give the stroke stronger accentuation, so that each stroke will exhibit a light and a shaded side.

Charge your brush as follows: clean the brush and put it sideways into the heap of paint. Then, when you draw the brush over the china, the colour will look strongest on the side of the china where the stroke began. This kind of stroke is called a fading stroke. When you charge the brush with paint in this way you can give shape not only to the strokes but to the entire motif. You thus give the effect of shadow.

On this ashtray the three strokes in the motif subject on the tile above are used, a couple of new types of strokes being added on the upper side to make the pattern more lively. Variety gives life! Several colours are used, another thing that gives life to the design.

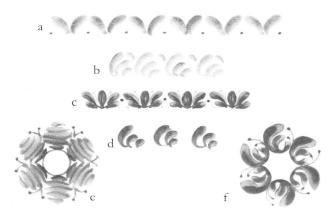

Some examples of accentuation; a and b are toning strokes, c and d shading strokes, e and f contouring strokes.

Shading

When you have painted the motif you can heighten the shadow effect by discreetly adding more paint to the shaded side, either the same colour or a darker colour. This second coat of paint, which beginners will find it easiest to apply when the motif has dried, is called shading. You will see very clearly when you work with fading strokes how the white of the china shows through where the paint is thin. China paints are glazing paints; that is, they are translucent. You can obtain a very light colour by dipping the tip of your brush in turpentine and drawing it through the heap of paint without stroking it on the edge of the turpentine cup. (For light and dark colours, see p. 33.) When you apply glazing paints one on top of another you always get a deeper tone, even if you use the same colour both for the first coat and for the shading.

Shading can create an effect of depth, but the effect must never be strong enough to become one of perspective. If you like naturalistic flower paintings as your motifs, then the shading is a means of obtaining depth. But the depth must as it were lie on the surface of the china – it must not give the impression that you are altering the surfaces by painting in perspective.

Put simply, we can say that depth merely gives a slight form to, for instance, a leaf without clashing with the rest of the painting, which we may call flat painting. It should also be said that if you are painting on a piece of curved china, any curve that you mark in your painting – whether it is a leaf or a flower – must always follow the shape of the china.

Perspective and Depth

The decoration of china is a flat art in which classic perspective has no place. Of course you do see perspective used on old pieces of china, especially those from the periods in the history of china when the art of decoration was at a low level, and when china was overdecorated. The best use of perspective was in miniatures, where the effect of perspective is not so striking.

A landscape on a teapot with mountains fading away into the distance can give the impression that, if you looked inside the teapot, you would find a whole range of mountains at the bottom. To put it simply, perspective makes bumps or dents on the china and that is why it is not appropriate in china painting. It is no defence of the use of perspective to say that you will find it used in motifs on china from certain periods. Not all old china is equally beautiful, and not all periods can boast a style of the same artistic quality, even if you do find specimens of them in the museums.

Rose by Karen Grip. The illustrations show the preliminary work on the combination of strokes for a rose, and the completed motif painted on a bonbonnière.

The Grey Colour Scale – Neutral Colours

In contrast to the strong colours we have talked about and used so far are the white, grey and black. They have no hue and are therefore called the neutral or colourless colours. These colours differ from one another only in their lightness or darkness: white is the lightest of all colours, black the darkest, while the many grey tones between white and black have an intermediate lightness. These intermediate tones can be made by mixing black and white.

You can get grey and black china paints, but not white. The lightening effect which, with other kinds of paint, you get by adding white to the colour has to be obtained in china painting by putting the paint on thinly (glazing), so that the white colour of the china shows through and takes the place of the white paint. This is called an optical mixture, in contrast to a mixture of paints, which is described as a physical mixture.

As mentioned above, the three primary colours and the secondary colours obtained by mixing them can be naturally arranged in a circle. But you can't make a similar circle out of the grey tone scale, because it has only the two main colours, black and white, the other tones in the scale all being mixtures of these two. The grey scale must therefore be represented by a straight line, with white and black at the opposite ends. (See the diagram below.)

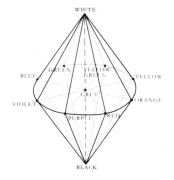

A diagram to illustrate the colour system.

Broken Colours

By mixing the strong colours with the neutral colours, you can obtain a large number of broken colours. These colours make up by far the largest number of the colours we see. An eye with normal vision can distinguish many thousands of different shades of colour.

If you are to handle the many colours and be able to work with certainty both with the mixing of colours and with composition, you need to know the basic colour system.

The Use of a Colour System

First and foremost, a colour system enables you to understand that the many colours that surround us and which we are more or less able to perceive are all mixtures of the primary colours with one another and with the colours on the grey tone scale.

The colour system illustrated on p. 49 shows how the six main colours are changed when they are mixed with given proportions of black or white. (This has been done here with watercolours.) You can make up and insert several circles in the chart according to the amount of black or white used in the mixture. You can gradually build up your own colour chart using both mixed and bought colours by painting a stroke on a tile or plate every time you paint with a new colour. Put the strokes round the radius of a circle, drawn in advance, each in the place you believe to be correct. This will help you, incidentally, to learn about colour families, which is the term for colours that are grouped round one principal colour and its neighbours, the most nearly adjoining colours.

You can go on making new colours from the six principal colours by mixing them in pairs, but you will find as you go on mixing that the colours gradually acquire more and more grey, even though you do not add any colours from the grey tone scale. This is another way in which broken colours are made. You will therefore find that in many cases the intermediate colours will be brighter if you buy them separately rather than making them yourself.

8. Marking and Drying the China

Marking

While the paint is still freshly ground on the palette it is a good thing to mark your name on the reverse side of the china. This is a great help to the firing centre, who have to see that things get back to their right owners. If you like you can write your name or initials with pencil first and then paint it in with paint. If you prefer to have your signature on the front, you must do it very discreetly so that it doesn't catch the eye. Any signature must always fit in naturally with the design. When china from a class is sent for firing all together, the best thing is to decide on a code, perhaps a number, to cover the whole batch.

Drying

Dry the china thoroughly after marking it so that it doesn't get scratched in transit. You can dry the painted china at room temperature, but that takes several hours. Most people therefore prefer to put the objects on a good warm radiator, if there is one available. That will reduce the time for drying to about an hour. China paints can also be dried in an electric oven with a thermostat set at about 240°F. (or 115° C. or in a gas oven at Mark $\frac{1}{4}$). In this way the time is further reduced, to about 15 minutes.

If the china is in the oven too long, or the temperature is too high, the paint may take on a brownish tinge because it will begin to burn on to the china. Don't be too worried about that; the right colours will appear when the china is subjected to the much higher temperatures of the kiln. What is worse is if the paints shrink and crack off through being warmed up too fast. If that happens there is nothing else to do but begin all over again.

Dust

You must be very careful that no dust gets on to the wet paint, both while you are actually painting and while the work is drying; after the firing, the dust will show as tiresome grey spots in the finished design. Small flat objects can be covered with an inverted plate or something similar, larger things with Polythene. Whatever you use for covering, it must of course never come into contact with the wet china paint.

It is best not to paint in a place with a woollen carpet, which will produce fluff, and the clothes you wear for painting must also be free from fluff. If you are painting at home, the kitchen is a good place to work in.

9. Getting Ready for Firing

Cleaning the China

Before you send a piece of work for firing you must clean off any spots of paint that do not belong in the design. Whether you clean it before or after drying is a matter of choice, but it is always easier to remove newly applied paint. If you dry the paint in an oven, it will be best to clean it before drying. Any surplus paint can be removed with a brush moistened with turpentine and then lightly dried. Where there is paint that touches the painted motif, be careful that you don't damage that.

If the paint has dried before cleaning, there are several methods you can use for getting the surplus off. One way is to roll a bit of cotton wool round the point of the brush-handle (use the pointed wooden kind) and moisten it with turpentine, with which you can wipe off the surplus. You can also use an etching pen (see p. 85) to scratch it away. The pen has other uses in connection with china painting which we will come to later. (See the passage on negative drawing on p. 84.)

Whether you do the cleaning before or after the paint is dry, it is as well to make a habit of polishing the surface of the china round the motif with a cloth moistened with spirit. There may be fingerprints which won't become visible until after firing.

Cleaning the Brushes

Do not forget to clean the brushes! If there is a bit of turpentine left in the cup, dip the brushes in it several times and then dry them carefully with a cloth. If the turpentine is getting thick you must wash the brush afterwards in spirit or the hairs will become stiff. You need not take the brush out of the handle each time you have used it.

To make sure you don't damage the brushes – especially when you have to carry them about – it is a good idea to cut out a little square of fluff-free cloth to roll round each one, but be careful that you don't bend the hairs. Brushes can also be kept on a piece of cardboard with a length of broad elastic sewn to it in which you can stick your brushes.

Properly handled, a brush will last a long time, and the advantage of that is not only economical. A brush wears with use, and it is easier to work with a brush that you have 'worn in' than with a new one.

Firing
For most paints the actual firing takes place at a temperature of about 1,500 °F. (815°C.) At this temperature the glaze on the china fuses and the china paints sink into the soft glaze and combine with it. After firing the glaze hardens again, and the paints are as it were protected by the glaze. The decorations you have painted yourself will therefore be just as durable as those on china bought ready-painted.

Electric kiln for china. The porcelain is stacked in the kiln ready for firing. In recent years many amateurs have got their own kilns, so that they can undertake intermediate firing, which is very useful when they are working on large, difficult tasks. Nowadays kilns can be obtained in various types and sizes; that shown here is called a K 180, which means that it has a capacity of 180 litres.

Paints that Change during Firing
There are some red paints that cannot be mixed with other coloured paints and cannot be fired at the temperatures normal for ordinary china paints. To save these red paints from disappearing during firing the temperature has to be not more than 1,418°F. (770°C.) Among other colours that alter in firing are the dark blue cobalt paints and the purple paints that contain gold. These paints need a firing temperature of 1,562°F. (850°C.) if you want them to come out bright.

There is no reason why you should not use the purple paints and the cobalt paints together with other colours and fire them at the normal temperatures, but if you do they will, unlike other colours, remain matt after firing. Also, if these paints are not fired at the higher temperature they will not withstand wear, and the motif must not be allowed to come in contact with anything acid like lemon juice, vinegar, fruit juice or tea, which will quickly cause them to fade. The reason for their lack of durability is that at the lower temperature the pigment does not fuse sufficiently for the paint to be combined with the glaze. In other words, the paint does not sink deeply enough into the glaze but lies on the surface of it. (See also the warning about poison on p. 4.)

You might suppose that you could fire all china paints at the higher temperature, but that doesn't work. The paints with the lower melting-point sink too deep in the glaze, which makes them light and pale.

However, as far as the durability of the paints with high melting-points is concerned, it is possible to improve things by adding a white glass powder, flux No. 40, to the paint mixture. The powder hastens the melting of the paint so that it combines with the glaze more easily.

Most china paints can stand being fired several times. If you are painting large and difficult motifs, therefore, it is a good idea to give them an intermediate firing. Be warned, however, against firing black paints more than twice; with a third firing they will generally scale and flake off, which can ruin not only your own painting but other things in the kiln.

10. White China

Before we go further with painting we ought to have a look at what china actually is.

China is a highly developed ceramic product. It differs from what is normally called pottery in its hardness, translucency and clear white colour. Pottery is, generally speaking, a term describing all products of burnt clay such as, for instance, delftware and earthenware.

China consists of three principal ingredients: kaolin, quartz and felspar. These are mixed together at the factory to form a mass which is then shaped into plates, dishes, cups and so on. When the china is shaped it is fired in a kiln heated to a temperature of 1,652°F. (900°C.). What you then have is a semi-manufactured article, which still has to be glazed and bright-fired. This last firing is done at temperatures between 2,450° and 2,650°F. (1,350° and 1,450°C.), and you then have white, undecorated china, ready to go on the market.

You will do well to use only good quality china, even though it is the most expensive. The glaze on cheap china may be of a quality that affects china paints, making them stay matt and lose something of their original colour.

China can also contain iron, which appears in the form of small dark brown spots. If you use this quality you will have to place your motif on the article in such a way that the spots are seen as little as possible. In good quality china the particles of iron are virtually all removed. The iron appears more or less all through the body of the china, according to the quality. The iron is eliminated in the factories either with magnets or by filtering.

If dark spots appear after the firing that is carried out when a motif is painted, they should not be confused with iron spots. In most cases they occur because the kiln has not been properly cleaned. Spots can also be caused by paint that has been applied too thickly flaking off.

If you buy seconds, make sure there are no small cracks or blisters in the material; cracked china cannot stand up to firing.

Delftware

Delftware is cheaper than china; the glaze is softer and the body is more porous than that of china. It is therefore easily scratched in use. However, with its coarser texture and consequently stronger shapes, it is suitable for stronger, more modern forms of decoration, and in the case of purely decorative objects such as vases it will not matter that it wears badly.

Delftware bowl. Delftware is better suited than porcelain to a coarse kind of decoration. In this case the large strokes are made up of several small strokes, but they can just as well be done with a bigger brush.

Delftware is sold with both a clear glaze and a cream-coloured glaze. The coloured glaze gives the china paints a brownish tint that most people would wish to avoid. This discolouration is due to manganese in the glaze. If you do use the cream-coloured material, you must apply the paints very thinly, which will prevent to some extent the shift in the colours. But red tones will always turn brownish in firing, however thinly you apply them. Purple colours will change least.

Four painted objects.

Attractive patterns can be developed with the use of lines. The first row shows some ideas for straight lines, the second row some possibilities using curves.

11. Making Patterns with Lines

Vertical, horizontal or oblique lines, of various lengths and at various distances apart, can make a simple starting-point for a design, as the lines can form a framework for applying the strokes.

The diagrams below and below left illustrate how you can make patterns on paper before painting them on the china. Patterns can be made out of quite simple lines, which take shape as you sit and play with them. Do the drawings on squared paper and sketch in the guidelines and strokes that you want on the china. You will need a pencil, ruler, felt-tip pen and loose-leaf sketch-block.

Figures with vertical axes.

Vertical Lines

The lines – vertical, horizontal or other – round which the designs are built up and which give them their vertical or horizontal character are called their axes. When you paint strokes along a vertical axis, as shown above you will perceive an upward movement in the design.

With a little imagination you will see that the three strokes that seem to grow up from the baseline give the impression of a simplified flower. When the flower is repeated a number of times, you have made a border. If you paint the upper strokes, say, yellow and the lower green, the effect of a flower is intensified.

Colour compass.

By varying the length and breadth of the strokes you can create simplified 'symbols' for different patterns and flowers. Erantis and crocus have been the starting-points here. By changing the colour in a motif you can give a pattern quite a different effect, just as you can by changing the strokes. For instance, you can give an impression of 'folk art' by painting the top strokes orange and the bottom ones blue. (See the coloured illustration on the front cover.)

Building up a design in which the vertical axes form the foundation.

The diagram above shows vertical lines in rising and falling lengths. The strokes, painted out from the lines so that they just touch one another, combine with the lines to make a pattern suggesting the branches of a row of bushes. It will seem natural to paint the strokes green, with a light colour above and a darker below, to emphasize the resemblance to bushes. A painting that uses the technique of tonal variation from light to dark is called a 'tone on tone' painting.

As a rule you will be able to 'frame' a design with lines that make up a geometric figure – a square, for instance, a triangle or a circle. Suppose for example, you build up a pattern of triangles on the outside slope of a plate or a dish; the triangles can help to make a regular division of the rim of the china. Also, the triangles can form a border enclosing the design on the surface. You will often find that a frame of that kind adds something new to the design or border and may form a part of it.

The use of lines can also give coherence to a border and enhance the effect. In such cases you can well let the guide-lines remain, as they are painted in with china paints. In the diagram below left, however, the triangles are intended purely as an aid in placing the design on the china. But you can leave the vertical guide-lines as the stems of the brushes, painting them in with a darker colour.

Horizontal Lines

In contrast to patterns that are built round vertical lines, the strokes here are built round horizontal lines.

In the diagram below three single strokes are repeated on both sides of the line. To prevent the pattern from getting monotonous two strongly contrasting colours are used. (For contrasting colours, see p. 32.)

Strokes built round horizontal lines.

Colour compass.

A motif painted in a single colour always looks restful so long as the drawing is also restful and uncomplicated. As soon as you add a new colour that goes well with the other, the effect becomes more lively. But if you use a lot of colours in a regularly repeated pattern the whole effect can easily get restless and unharmonious, even if the patterns themselves are attractive and simple. It is best to go to work carefully until you are familiar with colour combinations and tonal variations.

To create a pattern that fits in with a given object you have not only to choose between many possible ways of formimg and combining the strokes, but also to take into account the colours and colour schemes, and to be sure that the colour agrees with the pattern.

Even if the size and shape of the strokes are changed (see below), they are still attached to the horizontal line, the cross-axis. Such a pattern will often look best on oval articles or round a spherical object such as a jug or vase.

A pattern painted lightly, in light colours, will often look best if placed at the top of an object, while a pattern in dark, heavy colours will most often be best placed near the bottom of the china. The denseness of the drawing also makes a difference. The pattern shown below can be framed in a hexagonal figure.

A relationship pattern built on a horizontal axis.

The geometric frame that can encircle every design can also give you quite new ideas for patterns in conjunction with the lines on the squared paper. (See above.) It is a question of whether you should encircle the motif by drawing lines from one point to another or do it without guides and so save time. You can, however, use the lines as a skeleton for the final application of the strokes.

You can also repeat whole groups of patterns, creating a relationship with or without variation, vertically or horizontally, as the shape of the china dictates.

Crossed Lines

For the sake of clarity I have discussed patterns based on vertical and horizontal lines separately. But you will often see patterns composed along both at once, the axes forming a cross, one line of which is intended as an axis for correcting the pattern and placing it on the china, while the other acts as a support for building up the pattern.

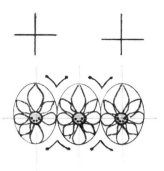

A design built on crossed lines.

You can shift the crossed lines in many ways. The diagram above shows an example of shifting, together with a design built up round it and repeated in relation. If the axes are not the same size it will generally be the longer one which dictates whether the pattern is extended horizontally or vertically – the dominating axis is decisive. But here too density of the design makes a difference, and so does the heaviness of the paint.

In the figures in this section you can see the starting-point and the preliminary work that preceded the sketches. The basic theme can of course be varied in many ways, for instance in:

the size and angle of the strokes
the distance of the strokes from one another
the placing of the strokes on the axis
the colour (one or more colours, use of fading
strokes etc.)

It is useful to know something about these principles of design and about short cuts for making patterns and borders. It is also important when you have to put a design on, for instance, a jug or some other piece of china with sculptural form; you will normally make the axis of the design follow the axis of the china, so that design and shape are in harmony. A tall, thin vase, for instance, will be dominated by the vertical axis, but a little stumpy jug is dominated by the cross-axis.

This 'line geometry' is our starting-point in the creation of designs which blend with the shape of the china.

12. Colours

Complementary Colours

If you stare at a strong colour, say red, and then shift your gaze to a white surface, you see a new colour, in this case green. This new colour, or after-image, is called the contrasting colour of the original colour. If you experiment with the other two primary colours you will find that the contrasting colours of yellow and blue are violet and orange, respectively. These pairs of colours are called complementary colours. The appearance of the after-image is due to a reaction in the optic nerve: the eye becomes tired if it looks too long at the same bright colour.

The three contrasting colours are the same colours that result when you mix the primary colours together in pairs. In a colour system, therefore, they appear opposite the colours that they are most remote from and to which they are complementary. (See the colour chart on p. 49.) This is true not only for the primary colours, but also for all the colours included in the main circle of the colour system.

When a pair of complementary colours is used together in a painting each throws the other into prominence, with a rather overwhelming effect on the eye; if the two colours are used in equal quantities on the surface they may seem to flicker.

The distance between colours is known as the degree of contrast. The greatest contrast occurs when you put together colours which are immediately opposite on the colour wheel.

If the colour combination is not made with knowledge and experience of colour effects, it can absolutely ruin a piece of work, no matter how beautiful the motif is otherwise. So it is important, when you are using complementary colours together, to use each one carefully and with due regard to the other. To get good combinations of these strong colours, as indeed with all colours, you must learn to balance them. For instance, one main colour can be combined with two weaker broken colours derived from the contrasting colour. You should make other experiments to take this further, in theory as well as in practice.

If you combine complementary colours by grinding them together, you will find that the reverse of what is described above will happen: the colours will be relaxed, i.e. will lose some of their colour, and all you will get will be a greyish brown.

As a beginner it will be best for you to paint in a single primary colour, varying it from light to dark. When you have had enough practice in the use of one paint in a number of tones you can increase your palette by the addition of the neighbouring colour, until at last you can embark on using contrasting colours together.

Warm and Cold, Near and Distant Colours

Most people will think of blue as a *cold* colour and of yellow, orange and red as *warm* colours. The cold colours are grouped round blue and green-blue in the colour-circle, the warm round red-orange, which is of course the typical 'fiery red'. The intermediate areas on the circle can be called the *temperate* colours. It follows that if you stick to, say, blue tints in painting china you will get a predominantly cool effect. But you can rectify the balance of colour by adding a warm yellow to the painting. It is not always the amount of the added warm colour that will make the difference, but the placing and strength of it. The greys are neutral, but they can be made to look either cool or warm. You can transform a motif that is either too cold or too warm by shading it with warm or cold colours.

Colours also have an optical property. They can as it were stand out from one another. Even if they are painted on the same surface you will notice that one colour seems to lie above the others and to be nearer you. These are *near* and *distant* colours. As a general rule warm colours look nearer while cold ones look more distant. But the effect also depends on the relative sizes of the painted areas and the concentration of colour. Artists make use of this effect, but it is hard to find a use for it in painting china, where the motif should ideally lie in the same plane without any strong perspective effect.

Light and Dark Colours

Two squares are shown below, each with another square inside it. In the first example we have a white square with a black background, in the other a black square with a white ground. You will notice at once that the white square on the black ground looks bigger than the black square on the white – although in fact the small squares are exactly the same size. This is due to a relationship known as 'eclipse'.

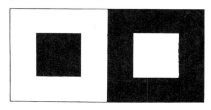

The same thing happens when designs are scraped out on a ground. It is like a stain on a light-coloured carpet; it is more noticeable than a stain the same size on a darker, patterned carpet. You will find that you can control the whole impression by means of light and dark colours.

If your first coat has been painted too dark there is no need to paint it all over again; simply shade it down with a really deep tone. The colour interval that results makes the undercoat appear lighter. You can use a trace of brown or black to get the shading colour dark enough. If an undercoat looks too light you can shade it down gradually – if you do it too abruptly the interval between the colours will be too great and the undercoat will look even lighter. In painting flowers a dark paint used for the veins and, if necessary, the outlines can make the whole painting look darker.

Be very careful about the use of black in shading light colours, as the paints easily get a muddy look. It is best to do without black altogether. If the surroundings are themselves very dark, you may have to use black to get a deep enough tone. In the darkest range of colours there is less risk of the paints looking muddy.

Your exercises in colour mixing will be of help here, as you must always try to get the right interval between the colours.

It is exciting to experiment with mixing colours; you are continually undergoing new experiences. You can arrange your own mixtures in a painted colour chart of your own, as discussed on p. 9. And you will of course learn from your mistakes.

As has been mentioned before, not all paints can be mixed together, on account of their chemical composition, so there will still be certain colours that you will have to buy instead of making them yourself.

13. First Drawing with a Pen

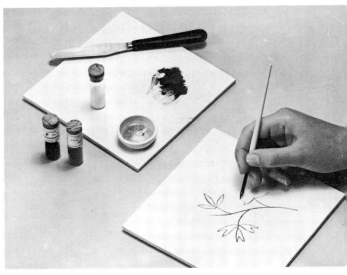

Drawing with pen and sugar paint.

Before we go on to painting large motifs let us have a look at how a pattern can be executed in china paint. This way of executing the pattern has the advantage that the drawing of the motif will remain even if you have to wipe off the paint because something has been painted wrong, whereas pencil lines will disappear. It is therefore a specially good process for beginners.

In addition to a drawing pen (see list of materials on p. 13), you will also need:

    1 part light grey
    $\frac{1}{4}$ part icing sugar
    a few drops of water

Sugar acts as a binding agent, making the paint cohere. For pen drawing, therefore, you can use sugar instead of oil.

First take a little powder with the spatula, enough to cover about 4mm. ($\frac{1}{8}$in.) of the tip. Put this on a mixing tile which has been cleaned off with spirit and add about 1mm. of icing sugar with the spatula, with a drop or two of water. Granulated sugar can also be used, but it is not so easy to dissolve in cold water.

Grind the mixture thoroughly and add a few more drops of water so as to produce a drawing paint that is quite fluid. You can test the consistency of the paint by drawing with it on the mixing tile. Turn the pen upside down, dip it into the paint and fill it like a shovel.

When the time comes to draw, turn the pen right side up again, but if you are using icing sugar you must hold the pen more horizontally than you would for writing. The drawing is done quite lightly.

If you are good at freehand drawing you can do without the preliminary freehand sketch in pencil, and draw directly with the pen.

The following rules apply to pen drawing with powder paints, icing sugar and water:

(1) Drawing is best done on a surface that has been rubbed with spirit and completely dried.

(2) The drawing must be done with light, thin lines, preferably with light grey paints, since these give the most attractive results. A dark outline may well ruin the final work. For drawing black motifs, see p. 36.

(3) If the drawing goes wrong you can 'rub out' the mistake with water. Take care not to touch the drawing with your fingers. The least bit of warmth or moisture from your hand is enough to ruin a drawing even when it is quite dry.

(4) The finished drawing can be dried on a radiator. It dries within a quarter of an hour and is then cooled off.

(5) The dry and cool drawing is highly resistant to turpentine, which has the advantage that you can very easily wash off graphite and other impurities with a cloth dipped in turpentine.

(6) When the china is fired the pen drawing will remain.

All tones of colour can be used with the sugar mixture described here. The motif on the schnapps bottle is drawn in a deep blue-green colour.

(7) If the pen will not work properly, it may be due to lack of practice. It is not easy to draw with a pen on china, yet it is a process you can learn relatively quickly. The cause may of course be of a technical kind:

(8) The nib opens – you are pressing too hard on the china.

(9) Dirt in the nib – if a pencil has been used, this may be due to graphite from the pencil or the tracing paper used to transfer the motif. Clean the pen with water and a cloth.

(10) The pen slips on the china – probably due to the china's being damp. Dry it more thoroughly.

(11) The paint separates or the drawing looks woolly – there must have been some oil or turpentine left in the cloth the china was dried with. Rub it over with spirit and start again. It is a good idea to have several small cloths ready for use.

You can easily clean the tile and brush for this drawing paint with water. Rinse them with spirit afterwards. (Make a habit of this.) This last cleaning is important if paints are going to be ground with turpentine immediately afterwards.

If in spite of every precaution the pen drawing still looks a little bit uneven, don't despair. When the drawing is dry you can go over it again with an etching pen (it fits into an ordinary penholder) and scratch out the parts where the line is uneven or too thick, When the paint is still wet you will also be able to make corrections with the tip of the brush-handle.

You can draw over lines sketched in pencil, but not over a drawing done with the All Stabilo pencil, which will make the drawing pen slip.

First drawings with sugar paint may look a bit heavy as a result of the hard outlines; in particular, the motif is completely enclosed where perhaps there really ought to be only an outline on the shaded side. However, many beginners will be glad of the backing given by a strong line. And if for any reason you have to wipe off the paint and start again, you will always have the basic drawing left.

Beginners and more advanced painters alike will find

in this form of preliminary drawing a good, sound support when they want to try out different colours on one of their own designs.

Drawing in Indian Ink

You can also use Indian ink for the preliminary drawing of motifs. The fountain pens specially designed for Indian ink can be recommended here. Generally speaking, Indian ink has the same advantages as the drawing paint described above, in that it is not destroyed by turpentine and can be washed off with water. Indian ink can be thinned with water if desired.

But – in contrast to the paint drawing – Indian ink disappears in firing. When you come to put on the paint, therefore, paint over the black lines, especially at points where two colours meet, otherwise there will be a streak of white in between them. And where the outline is meant to be prominent, you must give it a touch of paint.

14. Motifs in Black – Silhouettes

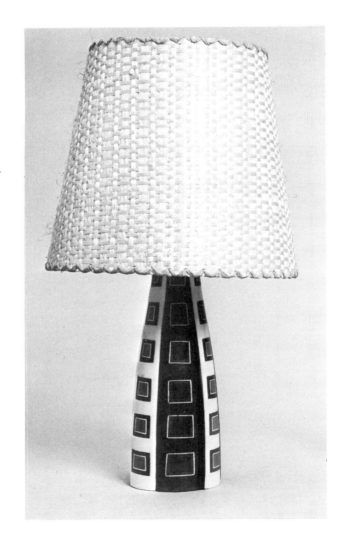

The folded paper cut-outs corresponding with the squares on the lamp form the basis of the lamp's decoration. Draw the same squares in the working binder, then play around with the cut-out squares until you have worked out a suitable pattern.

The white china is covered with plastic tape and then treated with a ground. Scratch out the white squares with an etching pen.

You can apply a new colour after intermediate firing.

It virtually never happens in a china painting class that all the students get on at the same pace. And that is just as it should be. Each must work at his own rhythm. Perhaps there will be some waiting for an intermediate firing, or for help from the teacher, so it is convenient to have some tasks that can be used for filling in time. Among such are black motifs, which can be extremely attractive, and which will also appeal to the student who is following the book by himself.

Black is gratifying to work with. The strokes generally fire to an even overall result even if they have not been applied quite evenly (though of course you should always try to avoid that). People often say that black is difficult to paint with, but so long as you have learnt to use it properly the difficulties can be overcome. So there are several reasons for keeping yourself occupied with work in black.

Preliminary Drawing

The motifs reproduced here in silhouette are suitable for small (quarter-size) tiles. To begin with you are advised to confine yourself to painting on flat surfaces; later you can try with ash-trays, vases, cups, ornaments and so on.

For the pen drawing of the outline you need:

1mm. black
1mm. light grey
$\frac{1}{4}$ part icing sugar
water

Grey is added to the paint for the drawing because black separates when it comes in contact with water unless it is mixed with another colour.

Draw the outline of the motif on the tile with a pen, then dry it on the radiator for a quarter of an hour. Meanwhile grind the black colour for filling in the drawing.

Putting on the Black Paint

For this, you grind:

2mm. black
plus oil and turpentine

For silhouettes – and indeed for other black motifs –

you should use oil sparingly; the less oil you use the darker the coat of paint will be. Black must never be too oily; use only the exact one-half part of oil.

First coat – begin painting at the top left-hand corner of the motif so that you don't put your hand on the wet paint. Make the strokes overlap a little. Paint details with the side or the tip of the flat brush. With the first coat the result will not be absolutely black, but a grey-black, so the motif must be painted over again. But first you must dry the tile for an hour. Meanwhile cover the mixing tile with the rest of the black paint so that it does not gather dust.

Second coat – use the same paint as for the first coat, but if you don't return to the work until the next day you will need to grind the paint again with turpentine and a trace of oil. Paint that has stood a long time needs care in use – it can be 'troublesome'.

If the paint does not cover properly the second time it may be because it is too oily. A third coat will do no good, since too thick a coat of black paint easily flakes off in firing; the firing centres dislike little bits of paint from one object settling on others in the kiln, making black spots that cannot be removed. The same is also true if there is too much sugar in the pen drawing, so be careful both in mixing and in painting.

As will be seen, the difficulties of painting in black really lie in making sure that the desired black tone is obtained with the second coat, without painting too thickly or with paint that is too oily. If you don't get the right colour with the second coat, there is nothing to do but to start all over again. The pen drawing will remain when the paint is washed off with turpentine, and the catastrophe is thus of manageable proportions.

Black paint will not stand more than two firings. A third firing may cause the paint to flake off completely. Black is not advised as an outer rim, as it wears off.

Paper Cut-outs on China

Paper cut-outs painted in black on china can be extremely attractive and make it possible, among other things, to preserve children's cut-outs.

Fold a square piece of paper diagonally so that it

becomes a triangle. Fold over twice more, then make little cuts in the paper with a sharp pair of scissors and unfold the paper. The result is a decorative, symmetrical openwork pattern which can be traced either positively or negatively, by painting either the 'holes' or the paper round them, according to how the paper is cut. The effect is much the same as the Hans Andersen design right. The technique can also be used for working on grounds. (For grounds, see p. 78.)

Three cut-outs from Hans Andersen used for a children's party set on delftware, from the Royal Danish Porcelain Factory. The set is obtainable on cream, yellow and blue ground.

These three black motifs were carried out as silhouette cut-outs by Sofie Juel Bruun and reproduced from the book Tytte's Cat. The white spots and lines can be scraped out in the china paint with an etching knife.

Black

Never be afraid to start a piece of work again from the beginning. An extra effort, with a new coat of paint, gives both practice and experience, and it is the effect of the whole work that matters, not the time you've spent on it.

If black is considered a difficult colour, it is because this paint, on account of its chemical composition, is more apt to 'craze' in firing than other colours, if you have not worked accurately with it. If that happens and you can't repair the damage, then rub it all out. After a thorough cleaning to remove all traces of the rubbing, paint the spoilt part again and fire the china a second time.

This method of salvaging damage caused by 'boiling up' can also be used with other colours.

Silhouettes are 'shadow pictures' and must therefore be painted in the shadow's black colour. It is a complete misconception to paint silhouettes blue or red – they will be quite spoilt. If you really must use a colour, then it should be something so near black that it looks black or very dark.

15. Pen Drawing and Painting

A lot can be done with a pen

Pen drawing can be cultivated as an art form in itself, whether you are drawing a modest little motif or a large-scale decoration. It is not laid down anywhere that an embellishment on, say, a plate must be painted with a brush. Work done with a pen is in no way less fine than painted motifs.

Many modern artists have worked in pure line on china. Even if most of what you see in this field is printed from copper with a view to mass-production, its character is still the same.

Stylized paper cut-out snowflake, also suitable for negative line drawing on a ground (p. 84).

Transfer of Line Drawings

If you choose to transfer a motif rather than to draw it freehand, it is usually necessary only to draw the outline. The fine lines lying within the outline can be drawn freehand, so long as you have the 'frame' to guide you. But – `note that not every drawing has a true outline. The outline of the squirrel opposite right consists of a lot of little strokes, which look like fur. In such cases the outline must merely be suggested with little lines, both with the pencil and in the ink drawing.

The transfer of the line drawing can be done as follows. Sketch the design on a piece of transparent paper – graph tracing paper is the best for this. Then turn the paper over and shade closely all over the surface with a drawing pencil, first in one direction, then in the other. Now lay the paper on a china tile, cleaned with spirit and absolutely dry, with the shading

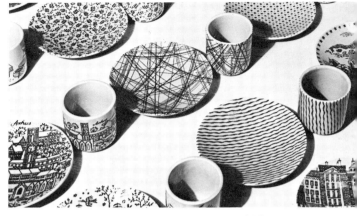

Line decorations on delftware carried out by Poul Hoyrup and Jacob E. Bang. The monochrome decorations are printed from copper in blue, red or green. Many effective decorations can be achieved with a pure line used as ornament or simple drawings made up only of lines.

A selection of simple motifs both for drawing and painting, well suited for beginners. These motifs, the work of Yrsa Wiff, were adapted for china painting and painted by a first-year student at an evening class.

downwards. Cut the paper round the motif so that it is not too big, and then fix it to the tile with a little cow-gum or some small pieces of Sellotape.

Follow the lines of the drawing with a hard pencil. The shaded side of the paper works like carbon-paper, so that the motif appears on the china in thin but quite visible lines.

Work on Drawing

A pen drawing will generally look best if it is all in one colour – that is, in *monochrome*. Choose the colour that suits the motif best – grey, brown or black. For the squirrel, the most natural choice will be brown. Of course you can use other colours for line drawings;

The models for these bird and animal drawings are a series of beautiful animal motifs that the well-known artist Leif Ragn Jensen has drawn and selected, giving particular attention to what is suited to china and what is within the capacity of beginners and amateurs. The motifs can be executed as pure pen drawings or as brush drawings.

thus a not too bright, broken red or green can look nice on china or delftware. For broken colours, see p. 25.

If a motif (as in the drawing of the squirrel) contains small, dark connected areas or shadows, they can be indicated by a suggestion of hatching painted in afterwards with drawing paint and a brush. The drawing paint covers the background and makes the area dark. However, drawing paint containing water can easily dissolve the underlying hatching, so it is not suitable for covering large areas. Instead, once the hatching is dry you can paint over it and shade with paint ground with oil and turpentine. If the brush has been used with the paint dissolved in water, it must be cleaned with spirit, since water and turpentine do not mix.

The pen drawing, like the silhouette, is very suitable for filling in time while the rest of the class is being instructed, or as a minor exercise to be done at home. When you have brought off your first successfully you can do several more in the same style.

41

16. Flower Painting

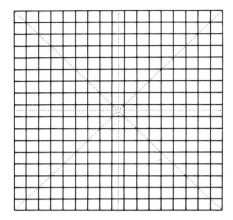

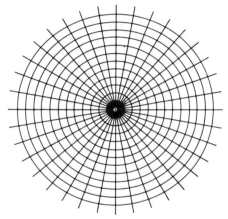

The Undercoat

Just because you have learnt your notes doesn't mean that you can play difficult pieces of music, and in the same way you can't start straight away on the difficult aspects of china painting even if you do know the fundamentals. You must practise the strokes again and again. The effect made by the stroke plays a great part in determining whether a decoration is beautiful or merely looks amateurish.

Even if you don't happen to be particularly interested in painting flowers, this subject affords good practice both in drawing and in painting.

If you have a flair for freehand drawing you can 'pluck' your subjects from real life – in fact, that is what gives the greatest pleasure of all.

Turn the china round while you are painting it so that your hand never touches it where it has already been painted, and so that the hand you are painting with doesn't have to be held in an unnatural position. You must always remember to rest any time you feel tense. If you are painting on tiles or other flat objects a wooden ruler with a pair of wooden blocks stuck on the ends will give excellent support for your hand. That way you will avoid putting your hand on the wet paint.

You paint flowers from the outside, by putting your brush down at the edge and 'touching' in towards the middle of the flower. If a stroke happens to cover the centre of the flower, which ought perhaps to be yellow, or indeed if you make any mistake in painting, you can lift the superfluous paint off completely with the aid of a brush moistened with turpentine and lightly dried with the cloth, from the handle towards the tip of the hairs.

Two simple aids which are of great practical value in drawing on angular and round things. The idea behind these devices is that china objects are placed on them so that guide-lines can be drawn over the china.

First, the tile divider (squared paper). When a tile is laid on the squares an exact guide-frame can be quickly drawn with an All Stabilo pencil. The tile divider can also be used for marking off tall rectangular objects. You can use loose sheets of squared paper as a tile divider.

Secondly, the circle-divider (circle-paper). It is used for cups, plates and other round objects with a border or other motif that has to be reproduced. Marks are set off on the article with the aid of diagonals. They can be extended if necessary. A bowl can be laid on the circle-divider bottom up and the marks set off on the outside. Guide-lines on the inside are marked by eye, working from the outside lines. Loose sheets of circle-paper can be used as a circle-divider. To mark off large articles you can use semi-circle-paper, in which case it will be best to glue the arcs together to make a big circle.

It is also a good idea to glue the divider to the underlay on which you work, so that it is always at hand when you want to mark off a piece of china.

Shading Blossoms and Leaves

Any paint left over on the palette should be covered to keep it free from dust, since you can use it later on for shading – putting in the shadows – when the motif is dry.

Because the transition from darker to lighter colours has to be gradual or 'blurred', most people tend to paint the shadows bigger than they really ought to be. You should therefore try to make the shadows a bit smaller than they appear to you. This is equally true for drawing on paper. If you are drawing from the living model you will often have to reduce the size of the shadows so as not to spoil the impression of the plant's juicy green colour.

(above)
Combining strokes to make flowers. Most of the petals are drawn in one stroke and then shaded after intermediate firing. The flowers and leaves take on their shape with the first shading, giving a three-dimensional impression of the plant.
(below)
Second shading must be relatively light and discreet. Besides correcting the first shading, it will further emphasize the shape.

If you painted exactly what you saw in the model you would have to put in all the ribs of the leaves. Such meticulous care would make the painting look wrong and unnatural. You should put in only as many ribs as are needed to make the leaf look natural, and those should only be suggested and not painted in all the way to the edge of the leaf. Another thing: you will notice that on the back of a leaf the ribs are lighter and more raised up than on the front, and that in real life there is a difference in tone between the two sides. You should therefore generally paint and shade the back side in lighter and cooler colours than the front. You must never paint or draw the ribs so that they dominate the painting at the expense of the leaf.

The undercoat determines the colour of the motif, and the shading must never completely cover the undercoat when you are painting flowers.

Some flowers may need to be shaded twice if they are to look really dark. In that case you can add a dark, neutral colour – grey, black or brown – to the first shading, and shade with it discreetly, taking care never to cover the first coat completely. A paint to which you have added brown, grey or black may make the colour of the flower or leaf look muddy.

The last shading gives greater depth and play to the colours. It also gives you a chance to make corrections so that the paints look right. Too strong a colour may stand out from the others and create a lack of harmony, but you can put that right by additional shading.

Shading means putting in the shadows; it is not until the flower motif has its shadows that it really comes to life. Flowers and leaves have character, and the shadows give them form and round them out. It is impossible to give firm rules on where to put the shadows. Just as the shadow moves over the face of a sundial from hour to hour, so the shadows on flowers change with the sun and with the position of the leaves and blossoms that cast the shadows.

Light Curves

A slight curve in a leaf or a flower need not be indicated when you put on the first coat of paint. First dip the tip of your brush in turpentine and dry it off slightly with a cloth, then 'pick up' the paint where the curve needs to be lighter. But you must leave a trace of paint, to indicate the shape.

A dark curve will depend on the amount of shading, with an extra coat of paint if necessary.

The Centre of the Flowers

The centre of many flowers is yellow. But yellow paints are very apt to get dirty, so let's examine how to get the best results with them.

You must grind them on an absolutely clean palette and with a clean spatula. A horn spatula is recommended, as metal ones may oxydize and give the paint a greenish tone. The brush, too, must be very clean, and you must make sure that the area to be painted is cleaned and free from bits of old paint.

It is best to let the paints you have already put on set and dry before putting on the yellow; you will have to wait five or ten minutes.

For the painting of stamens with relief paints, see p. 45.

More Delicate Pen Drawing – Details in Pen

In addition to the two forms of pen drawing described earlier, mention should be made here of a third, which can be recommended for drawing in fine details in a motif. The following materials are used:

4mm. ($\frac{1}{8}$in.) powder paint

a little more than half that amount of oil

1 or 2 drops of aniseed oil

The addition of aniseed oil holds up the drying, which makes the mixture specially suitable for drawing very fine veins, hairs on stalks, insects and lettering. With care it is possible to draw on a dry ground without intermediate firing.

During drawing the pen is held more vertically than if you were writing with it.

Any paint left over from drawing the motif can be used only if more aniseed oil is added to it. It does not matter if there is turpentine in the paint so long as there is not too much, in which case the line will not hold together. The drawing paint is *not* resistant to oil and turpentine, and so it will not be suitable for drawing a motif under a ground.

Painting of Stamens – Relief Paints

If a flower is to be painted with yellow or white stamens, then use a good yellow or white paint. These colours should be ground with less oil than other colours, so that they stand out a little (in relief) after they have been applied. These paints can also be ground with sugar and water and put on with a brush – but not too thickly or they will flake off.

The relief paint is put on with a long flower brush. It is painted as a raised, thin, semi-bright line.

17. The Meissen Method and the Berlin Method

The technique described so far is called the Meissen technique, after the famous porcelain factory (the oldest in Europe, founded in 1710). In the Meissen method, the paint has to dry before the shading is done. In the Berlin method, however, the undercoat and the shading take place in the same process – 'wet on wet'. The Berlin technique is therefore much more demanding than the Meissen one; if you start working on the Berlin technique right away, in the great majority of cases you will come to grief, particularly in a class, since the technique – as a technique for beginners – requires a great deal more personal supervision of each student by the teacher than there is generally the time or opportunity for. A large number of famous painting schools therefore begin with the far simpler Meissen technique.

The two methods lead to the same results in the end, but with the Berlin method you work more continuously and get a chance to see how the motif is developing on the china right away. Most advanced students will therefore sooner or later go over to the Berlin method, which with a practiced hand will give a 'softer' result. It is the subtly shaded and lively stroke that brings china painting to life, by an ability which requires constant practice with drawing and brushwork.

The Berlin technique can be carried out in two different ways. In the first, the undercoat is put on smoothly and thinly and a moment later – when the paint has 'set' – the shading is done on the wet paint. You have to have a very sure hand; it is not easy to correct mistakes, so you should make the blurred transition between light and shade straight away.

In the second process all the colours to be used in the motif are ground in advance – light and dark separately. Start by painting on the light tones, and then work outwards into the motif's darker tones, which are put on without waiting for the first coat to dry. You can also do it the other way round, from dark to light, a classic procedure in the art of painting which in the painting of china makes it possible to bring up all the light in the white colour of the china and produce a 'living' light.

For most people the easiest method is to begin by 'putting a bass to the treble' – putting shadows on the light colours. But whichever way you go about it, the distribution of light and dark colours is the decisive element in the result and in achieving the right balance of colours.

Paints are a demanding instrument to play on. Treble and bass must be mastered and played in proportion to one another – and there is no room for mere strumming! See also the colour lessons in the section on pp. 49–64.

18. Models

If you are of a romantic disposition you may happily go ahead with motifs of a romantic kind, but there are many ways in which you may go astray. It is amazing how much 'cosy romantic' stuff is produced by smart factories who churn out on their production lines bogus paintings of forest lakes and chalet-type houses, postcards with motifs dripping with sweetness and wall hangings of romantic castles.

There is nothing wrong with something being romantic, but it must be sincere and free from false sentiment and kitsch!

One of the aims of china painting should be to strengthen the feeling for quality, and with an instinct for the 'real thing' you will be able to avoid the pitfalls.

Decorative ornaments in present-day taste can be achieved by quite simple means. On the rustic-looking mug, an f-motif (see p. 105) is painted on a border left untreated when laying a ground on the rest of the mug. The highly simplified flowers are painted in red, violet and yellow colours.

Flowers from Nature

If you are painting flowers the best models will be found in nature. Take a sketch-block and perhaps some watercolours when you go out for a walk, and give yourself plenty of time, unless of course you are going to pick the flowers take them home, put them in water and paint them indoors. It is, however, better to sketch them out in the open, where you have the whole sensation of nature and where the plants can be seen in the actual shapes in which they grow.

Do not do your sketching only in summer. There are possibilities all the year round. There is richness, for instance, in the dried berries of late autumn, which look exceptionally decorative on china when painted in a

Winter Aconite (left, above)   Blue Anemone (left, below)
Coltsfoot (above)
When you have finished the first exercises in the book you should have acquired enough confidence to begin drawing sketches from nature. Here are three types of flowers which you can draw.

The sketches can be worked on at home to make them fit the chosen piece of china. The three paintings that follow show the results of such an excursion in search of flowers for use as motifs.

47

Winter Aconite flower and leaves, sketched naturalistically on paper within an oval, drawn freehand. After sketching a few flowers for practice, draw the flower on the china in pencil, first putting in the oval surround as a guide in transferring the motif to the cup. (For drawing on china in pencil, see p. 10.) Finally paint the motif naturalistically from the point of view of shape and colour.

The Blue Anemone here has an oval surround drawn with a stencil. As a starting point, divide the oval with a vertical and a horizontal line and draw the simplified flower over these.

Draw corresponding guide-lines on the china, then reproduce the flower round the bowl like a border.

A green paint is used, varied from light to dark shades – unlike the flower's natural colours.

The mid-point of the flower is painted yellow and the stamens in a white relief paint.

single colour (monochrome).

Draw the flowers from every side and make several sketches. It is a good thing to have some choice. Draw larger than life – the drawing can always be reduced. You should be able to give the feeling of whether the

Coltsfoot. After several rough sketches in fibre-pen on sketching-paper, and without the use of guide-lines, this flower is simplified until it becomes a stylized decoration.

When you put it on the china, first pad on the round centre part with a plastic foam pad and grounding paint through a circular hole cut in a piece of paper.

Grounding paint is paint that is ground with powder and oil, but no turpentine. You add a little over half the volume of oil that there is of powder paint. The mixture must be thoroughly ground before being padded on to the china.

For the paper with a circular hole, use squared paper of a suitable thickness with the circle drawn using a stencil over the printed squares.

The outline of the paper must not be cut too big, since the crossed lines drawn for guidance help with the placing of guide-points for putting on the rest of the decoration. The paper is stuck to the china with tape or green flower-wax. (For laying grounds, see p. 78.)

Plate 1 *Chart showing the reflection values of the colours and illustrating the distance between colours. The reflection value is the percentage of light reflected by the colours in proportion to white. The figures are approximate.*

The fifteen colours used in this book. The colours are shown as they look after firing, on the left with a single coat and on the right with two coats.

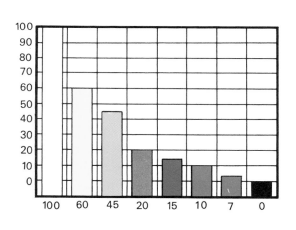

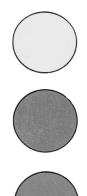

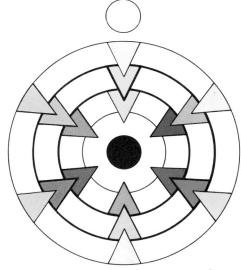

1. *bright yellow*
2. *dark yellow*
3. *orange*
4. *pale green*
5. *grass green*
6. *dark green*
7. *pale blue*
8. *sky blue*

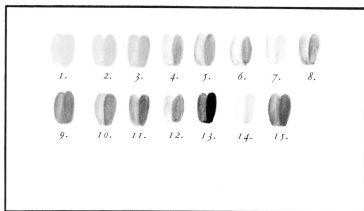

9. *red*
10. *scarlet*
11. *mauve*
12. *grey*
13. *black*
14. *pink*
15. *violet*

Plate 2 *Small motifs and scattered flowers*
Motifs of this kind, which are very simplified, are easy to begin with. They go well on small objects, and can be reduced further. (On reduction of motifs, see p. 103.)
(*a and c*) Yellow ear and yellow seed-pod. *The undercoat for both can be bright yellow, shaded with three parts dark yellow mixed with one part scarlet.*
(*b*) The red flower. *Use pink for the undercoat. For the brighter red petals use two coats of the same colour. For the brighter red petals use two coats of the same colour. For the centre, use grey plus pale green.*
(*d*) The blue flowers *can be painted with an undercoat of pale blue and shaded with sky blue.*

(*e*) The bud at the foot of the plate and the violet flower. *The undercoat for both can be one part pale blue plus one part violet. They can be shaded and outlined with the same colour plus a little black. Both buds are shaded with pink.*
Leaves. *Where the green colours are warm, use an undercoat of one part bright yellow plus one part light green. Where the colours are cool, use one part light green plus one part light blue. Shade with grass green plus dark green. You can vary the shading colours in the darkest places by adding violet or black. Touch up with a little orange. This applies to all the plates on which leaves appear.*

Plate 3 *Creeper*

A pen drawing with grey sugar paint is suggested for the first drawing of the leaves. Autumn leaves vary enormously in colour and must be painted in many shades. If you are following the model you can use for the undercoat colours that range from yellow, through yellow-green, to red and brown tints. Scarlet will do for the red. You can shade with the same paint deepened with darker colours. You should paint the stalks and berries with a brush without a preliminary pen drawing. Try to combine different shapes of leaves.

Plate 4 *Stylized bell-flower motif*

This bell-flower motif is shown here as a wreath but could equally be drawn in a chain. The whole impression depends on the tightly composed lines being absolutely firm, so the outline should be painted first.

Stalks and leaves *can be outlined with a brush using dark green and shaded inwards from the point with a slightly lighter colour.*

The flowers *are outlined with sky blue and the undercoat is done thinly in the same colour. A stronger shade of sky blue is also used for shading.*

Plate 5 overleaf *Chains and wreaths of flowers*
This plate shows how small motifs can be built up to form borders and wreaths.
The yellow flowers *can be painted with light yellow and shaded with dark yellow mixed with scarlet.*

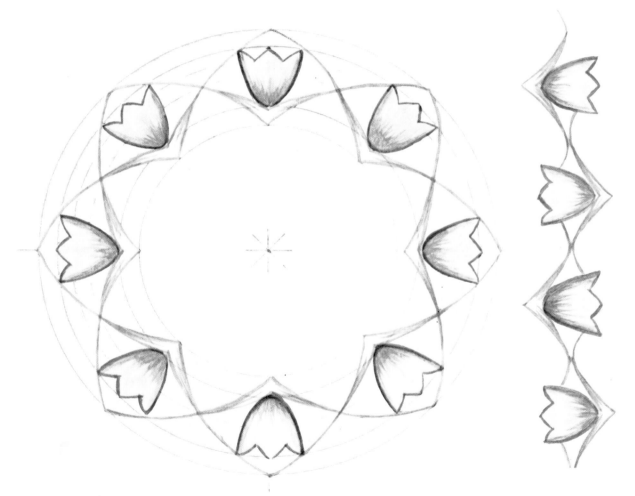

Red flowers. *For all of these you can use pink for the undercoat. For shading you can use the same colour mixed with either sky blue or violet, which gives a warmer tone. If you want a redder shading, you can use pink.*

Blue flowers. *For these you can use pale blue and sky blue. The same colours can be used for shading with the addition of mauve.*

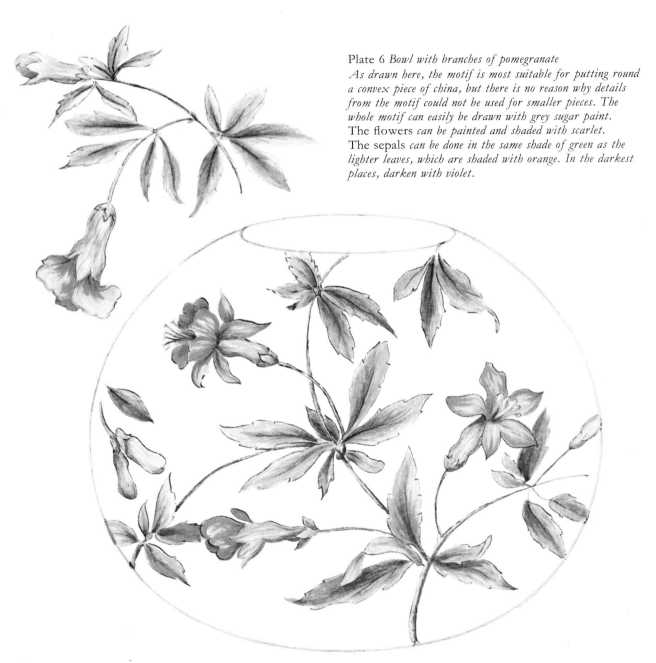

Plate 6 *Bowl with branches of pomegranate*
As drawn here, the motif is most suitable for putting round a convex piece of china, but there is no reason why details from the motif could not be used for smaller pieces. The whole motif can easily be drawn with grey sugar paint.
The flowers can be painted and shaded with scarlet.
The sepals can be done in the same shade of green as the lighter leaves, which are shaded with orange. In the darkest places, darken with violet.

Plate 7 Bouquets of flowers

The motifs on this plate can be used as a basic pattern for decorating sets.

The big motif is suitable for an oval piece of china, but of course it can be adapted to fit other shapes.

The flowers can be painted in a reddish tone as they are here, or in a light yellow. If you choose red, you can use scarlet for the undercoat. Go over the light surface of the petals with a thin gleam of orange plus pink. Shade the flower with the colour used for the undercoat. If you are using yellow, light yellow is recommended. These light surfaces should be painted very delicately so that the china can be seen through. You can do the shading with orange plus a trace of grass green.

The seed pods and the golden leaves can be undercoated with orange plus a trace of violet. The violet can be used for shading.

You can do the undercoat for the seeds with pale blue plus a trace of mauve. Shade with mauve. A little of the green leaf colour mixed with sky blue can be painted on the pod.

Plate 8 *Fantasy flowers*
Fantasy flowers go well on tea or coffee sets. Work on the motifs in your working binder until they fit the different pieces in size and shape. Since these are imaginary flowers, you can change the colours round as you like (while taking account of the colours on the table-cloth and other surroundings). The motifs can also be painted on cream-coloured china in the colours used here (violet, mauve, green, yellow and yellow-brown).

Plate 9 *Branch of forsythia*

The forsythia grows like a tree, making it suitable as a
motif for use on tall objects such as vases and lamp-stands.
The branches should not be bent into an unnatural shape that
will not accord with the way they grow.

You can also build up a decoration above the branches that
hangs down from the upper side of the object.

You should sketch the whole motif lightly in pen using
light grey sugar paint.

For the petals, *use light yellow for the undercoat and shade*
with the same colour or with the somewhat warmer darker
yellow, with a spot of orange or grey here and there.

For the leaves and sepals *use light green plus grass green*
for the undercoat and shade with the same colours. For the
darker areas, mix in a little grey. You can paint the ribs
with the shading colour, adding a little violet in certain places.
Where the stalks are still green, you can paint them in the
same colour as the leaves. Where they are woody, go over the
paint with violet, shading with the same colour.

Plate 10 *A spray of larch*

The red cones *are painted first with pink and shaded with the same colour mixed with a little sky blue. The underside of the cones and* the yellow-green needles *are painted first with bright yellow and grass green. Shade with grass green, adding a little black in certain places. The blue-green needles are painted first with dark green plus dark blue, and then shaded with the same colour plus a little black. The male cones and stalks are first painted with a bright yellow plus violet, and then shaded with the undercoat paint plus a little black. The outlines of the shells of the cones can be drawn on the dry paint with a very fine pen drawing using pink shading paint mixed with aniseed oil. It can also be done with a very fine brush.*

Details from the branches can be used for smaller things, or you can experiment with putting the branches together in different ways.

Plate 11 *Triangles* (Opposite)
(*a*) *The triangles form a tree, which has red berries. The triangles 'fly'—they move in the direction in which they are pointing.*
(*b*) *The pattern is a light and airy blue, which fits well at the top of the narrow jar. The lines round the object are drawn in All Stabilo pencil with the help of a banding-wheel.*
(*c*) *At the bottom of the pattern there are dark, and therefore heavy, triangles, which point down. The motif is*

a

b

c

d

e

f

rightly placed at the bottom of the vase, on account of its weight.

(d) Flat triangles against one another form a rectangle, which corresponds with the broad 'rectangular' shape of the jar, creating harmony between form and decoration.

(e) A few exactly fitting triangles are made into squares. Light green meets medium green, and medium green, dark green. There is room for an invisible square in the space between the base of the jar and the motif. Put a piece of squared paper round the jar and measure out how many squares are needed to go round.

(f) All the triangles point to the right; you follow the pattern round the vase as if you were reading. All the vertical lines must be exactly drawn. Triangle must touch triangle in at least one place or the motif will not hold together.

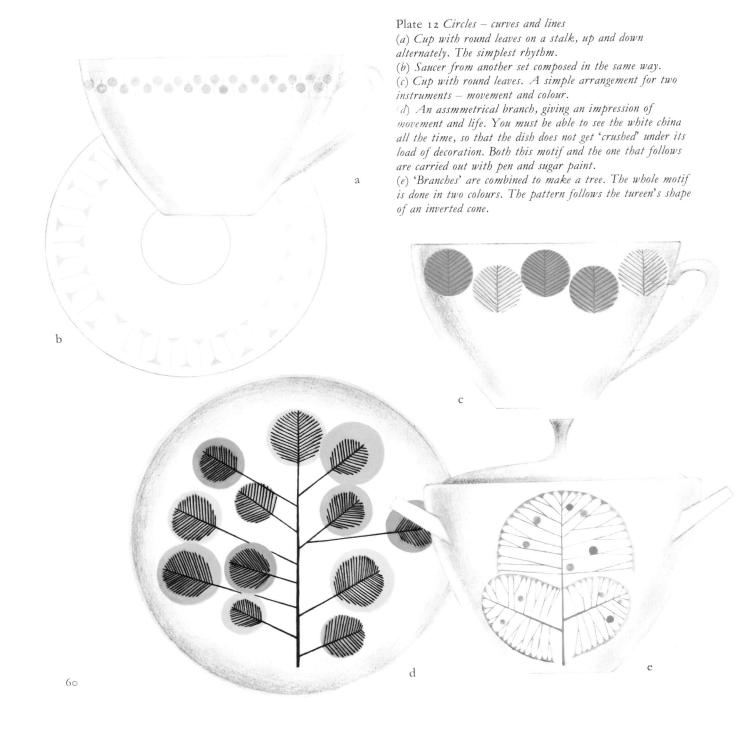

Plate 12 *Circles – curves and lines*
(*a*) *Cup with round leaves on a stalk, up and down
alternately. The simplest rhythm.*
(*b*) *Saucer from another set composed in the same way.*
(*c*) *Cup with round leaves. A simple arrangement for two
instruments – movement and colour.*
(*d*) *An assmmetrical branch, giving an impression of
movement and life. You must be able to see the white china
all the time, so that the dish does not get 'crushed' under its
load of decoration. Both this motif and the one that follows
are carried out with pen and sugar paint.*
(*e*) *'Branches' are combined to make a tree. The whole motif
is done in two colours. The pattern follows the tureen's shape
of an inverted cone.*

a

b

c

d

e

Plate 13

(*a*) *The composition of the pattern on this vase is based on three circles. The circles can be drawn either with the aid of a stencil, or with a banding-wheel.*

(*b*) *This beaker is quite simple – a border of squares and a ground.*

(*c*) *Falling leaves. The easiest way to compose a pattern like this is to cut out small squares of paper and arrange them on a sheet in your working binder. Beginners are advised to draw the small squares first in sugar paint (which remains during firing), or better still in Indian ink, which disappears in firing.*

(*d*) *For this model (and also for the other two tureens), you have to use a piece of measuring paper laid round the tureen so that you can work out the size of the squares.*

(*e*) *The 'brick pattern' on this tureen is the simplest pattern with squares you could think of.*

(*f*) *The last tureen differs from the previous ones only in that two colours are used and the motif is printed lower down.*

a

b

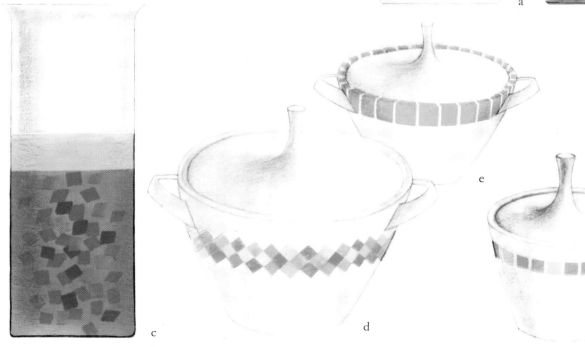

c

d

e

f

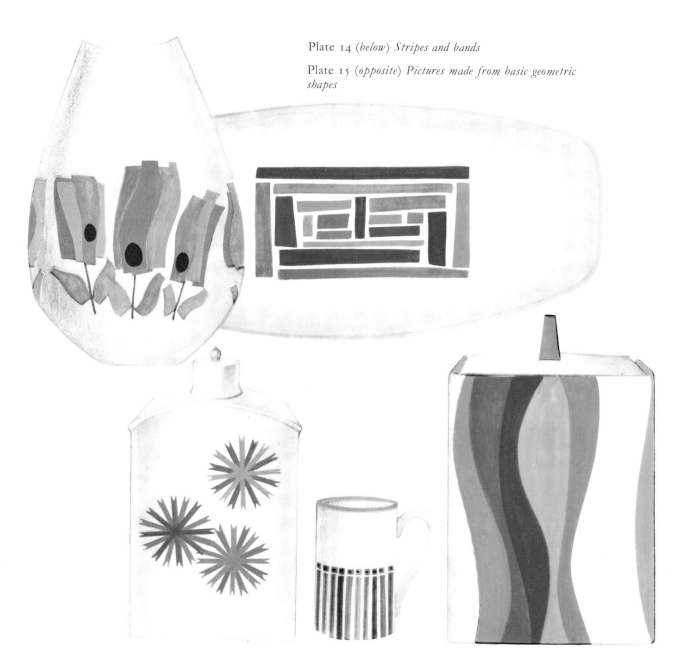

Plate 14 (*below*) *Stripes and bands*

Plate 15 (*opposite*) *Pictures made from basic geometric shapes*

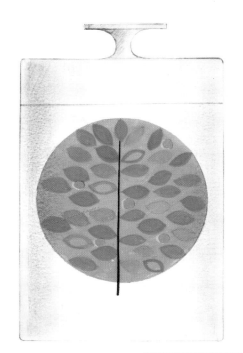
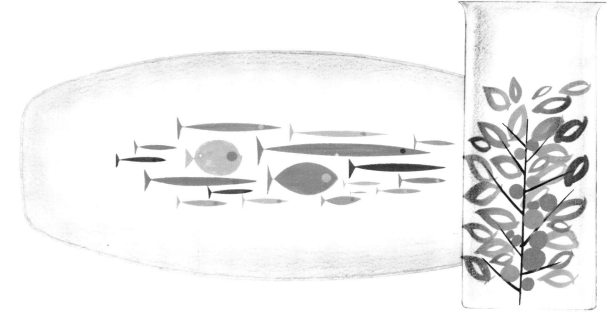

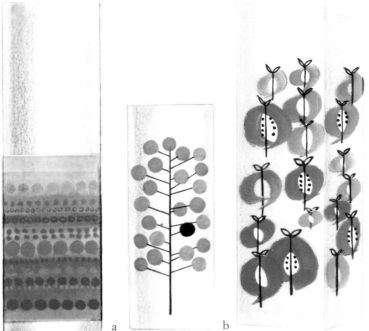

a

b

c

d

e

f

Plate 16 *Circles and spheres*

(*a*) *Note carefully that it is only an exact half of the vase that is decorated. Lay a ground first, growing lighter from bottom to top. Over this, paint belts of circles. Draw the circles first in Indian ink, using a curved stencil, then paint them after the ground has been laid. Indian ink will disappear in firing.*

(*b*) *The 'circle tree' is harmonious and balanced, even though there are more leaves on the right than on the left. Note that the branches only start to go out from the trunk about the centre of gravity of the vase. You can draw the branches with brush or pen.*

(*c*) *Seed-pods in two strokes. It is the stroke with character and life which gives this pattern so much of its effect. Draw the leaves and the black lines in pen or fine brush-strokes.*

(*d*) *'O-balls' like these are drawn freehand, in the form of a natural, unforced flower border.*

(*e*) *Big and little balls. It doesn't matter what they look like, so long as they are decorative and expressive.*

(*f*) *Spontaneity. More balls – but here they are shapeless and blurred. They change their nature – become fantastic flowers from an exotic paradise, when you take a brush and sketch petals or starfish in the middle of a few of them.*

stalk is hard and angular or soft and pliant, whether the leaves are smooth or rough, whether the flower is light or heavy.

To back up the sketches you can if you like draw guide-lines in the form of a square round the estimated outer points of the motif. First do a rough sketch of the flower so that the stalks and the position of the leaves are made clear. The whole must not be lost on account of the detail.

Think more about the flower you are drawing than about the china that the flowers are destined for. Of course if it is necessary for decorative reasons, you will always be able to invent new leaves and suppress others, or make any other alterations.

Paint the flower in watercolours and try to get as near to nature as possible. Watercolours can be mixed until you get just the right shade, so do not buy a paintbox with an enormous number of colours. Buy good quality, and be sure they are not poster paints. Also, get a few marten-hair brushes.

When the 'home-made' motif is there on the china

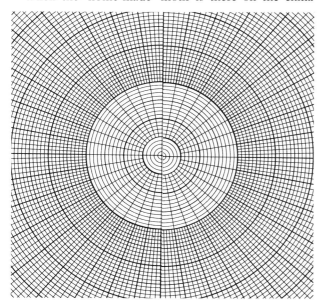

Roses have a reputation for being difficult to paint, but the problems can be overcome with practice. There are many ways of painting roses, and no one way can be recommended more than the others.

However a few basic rules can be given. Preferably paint from life. Use a tile to practise on, or the paper shown on left, and use only one colour. Begin at the centre of the rose and then lightly shape the rounding and the outer petals.

The fully rounded shapes result exclusively from the brushwork, which must follow the curves of the petals. On the light side, if the colour of the china is to remain wholly uncovered dip the brush in turpentine and take up the paint. Last comes light shading, which must be as simple and airy as possible.

The real difficulty in painting roses lies in making them as light as possible, and that is achieved only by using the white colour of the china as an element of the painting.

65

D

the painting becomes a real joy, and every teacher can tell of pupils who discovered a talent for drawing that they had no idea they possessed. Indeed, a drawing class will be well worth while for anyone who paints china.

Stylization
With stylized motifs we come nearer to personal expression. They are just like handwriting. A child's writing is a copy, or an attempt at a copy, of the writing of his teacher or that in the copybook. When the child reaches the years of discretion his writing becomes personal. The letters take on varied forms and are simplified – the handwriting is stylized. In the stylized motif you use your imagination to help make things personal. (See p. 76.)

Small Motifs and Geometric Patterns
We are surrounded by small decorative motifs that can be used for china painting: a detail from an old carved

Birds, copied from Dutch tiles. (Tønder Museum.)

chair or table, a little decorative part of a flower on a carpet, an illumination from a book, a sandstone ornament on the façade of a house and so on. If you keep your eyes open you can find countless small motifs which you can either develop or use as they are. Make a drawing of them when you see them – and keep a look-out all the time. (See also the section on p. 104.)

Children's Drawings
It can be amusing to put on to china drawings which the children in the family have done. Children's drawings nearly always have a strong decorative effect. Children have not yet learned the limitations, the agony of the irrevocable line – we who paint china could learn a lot from them about freshness and taking advantage of the

A child's drawing done by a five-year-old is transferred to the plate and drawn in one colour, retaining all the child's direct use of line. The cow was drawn by an older boy using china paints directly on to the mug.

66

fleeting joy of creation. Another thing: children – until they have learned about perspective – draw flat, without depth, which is particularly good for china. Give the children a cardboard plate and tell them to paint some suitable 'painting' on it with poster paints or tempera. A pencil is not a very good thing for smaller children to draw with because of the poor mark it makes, nor are wooden coloured pencils.

It is the simple directness of children's drawings that makes them what they are, so do not overwhelm the drawings by too much fuss with the china paints. Let the scales remain on the butterfly's wings!

These motifs are copied from Danish museums and collections by Richard Gale; special attention is paid to the development of a strong and lively stroke, which is so important in the decoration of porcelain.

These modern china shapes, decorated with motifs in contemporary style, were painted by Richard Gale.

A Christmas cup from the days when there were fairies. The cup was produced by the Royal Danish Porcelain Factory about 1860 by the colourful painter Peter Møller.

Sets for Children

An amusing set can be made from children's own drawings, but it is also possible to use figures from the children's fairy-tale world. Choose only illustrations that are done with artistic sensitivity. A teddy bear is better and more lifelike than the stereotyped Donald Duck and other figures from film cartoons. Look at the picture books again, but skip the cheapest and worst of them!

Special Occasions

It can be a pleasant custom to use a certain set or part of a set on important days. A Christmas set can be made both stylish and beautiful if it is painted with Christmas roses or more lightheartedly with Christmas fairies. It all depends on your inclination and your intentions. Search for the classic fairy types in old books and certainly avoid copying the modern commercialized fairies or little fairies who look like pin-ups!

If four funny fairy plates are printed they can be used as a kind of Christmas calendar for a child. Start using a new plate each week. The plates can be numbered and mugs can also be used.

Easter and Whitsun offer similar opportunities for holiday sets.

Obviously you cannot fill your cupboards with huge numbers of different sets, but if you normally use a neutral-coloured set – perhaps a plain white one – for every day, a few painted pieces can give the table a little variety for special occasions.

Other Possibilities

If you have a summer house it will be fun to paint a set with bright and simple summer motifs – wild flowers found in the district, fishing boats slipping off out to sea, various kinds of grain, leaves from the trees that grow near by and so on.

If you regularly have friends in to play bridge or other card games, it would be an idea to make a special set for that – or just ashtrays for the card-table. You can make lovely china paintings out of knaves, queens and kings – with a little talent for drawing you can draw them 'full face'. There would not be much fun in just painting diamonds, spades, hearts and clubs.

These are just a few ideas – the best will probably be the ones you think of yourself.

Part Two

Materials for Part Two

For Part Two of the book the materials listed below will be used in addition to those used in Part One. There is no need to obtain all the materials at once, but only as the need arises.

1 sketch-block with rough paper
1 box of coloured pencils that make a good, strong line
1 grounding brush
1 or 2 pieces of foam rubber with skin
1 thin foam rubber underlay about 30cm. × 40cm. ($11\frac{3}{4}$in. × $15\frac{3}{4}$in.)
1 sponge (natural washing sponge)
1 china painting brush
1 piece of blackboard chalk
1 etching pen
1 bottle of aniseed oil
1 bottle of ground-laying oil
1 pair of compasses, suitable for pencil or brush
1 packet of gold underlay
1 flower brush
1 horn spatula
Cow gum
1 reel of red Sellotape or other adhesive tape

The materials are listed in the order in which they are used in the book. Materials for working with gold are not included here but a list of them will be found on p. 107.

The paints suggested for broadening the range of your palette are included in the relevant section but not in this list. The same is true of the requirements for lustre paints.

19. Positioning the Motif

When an artist is about to make a drawing he is faced with a whole series of choices. He must choose the motif, decide what paper it should be drawn on with regard to thickness, size and quality of surface, and select the drawing materials best suited to the motif and to the paper – pen, brush, pencil, chalk or charcoal. And when all that is done he must decide how the motif is to be placed on the paper, whether the horizon should be high or low, whether the motif should be concentrated or spread out, and so on. None of these choices is accidental. They are determined by the artist's experience and knowledge of materials and the effects produced by them.

Similar choices lie before you when you paint china.

To write about such things in a few pages is very difficult. It is only too easy to be simple and crude, or to leave some possibilities out. What follows must therefore be taken as no more than an attempt to draw up a few guiding principles. And even so these observations must be taken with some reservation, since the real artist will break all rules.

Principle One

When a motif suitable for china painting has been chosen, the first thing that affects its placing is its size and 'weight'. It goes without saying that a little nosegay will look absolutely lost if it has to stand by itself on a large fish-dish. The motif is too light and slender. On the other hand, a heavy branch of an apple tree laden with ripe fruit will crush a coffee-cup if it is painted on it!

One motif can be big, another small. They can be powerful or slight. One motif can be light and airy while another of exactly the same size may be heavy and forceful-looking.

Colour, of course, also plays a part. For instance, a yellow colour has a light effect and dark colours make the motif heavy.

Principle One therefore works out as: *The size and weight of the motif, both in drawing and in colour, must be balanced against the size of the china it is painted on.*

A North Persian polychrome dish from about the year 1600. Note how the simplified flower and tree motifs fit into shape and emphasize its roundness. The eye is led naturally round the motif, beginning at the thickest part of the trunk, gliding up along the branches and following the motif round to the right. (Victoria and Albert Museum).

Principle Two

When you are sure that the motif and the china fit one another in 'weight and size', you must try to be clear about another important question: does the motif also fit the *shape* of the china? If we are talking about a flat tile there is no great problem. But when the china has curves – a sculptural form – it immediately becomes more difficult.

71

Principle Two runs: *The motif must follow the curves of the china.*

On a china object curved outwards (convex) such as a vase or a mug, the motif must fit in with the round shape and lie close in to the form. As an example of this, take a branch motif. If it appears from the drawing that the branch is straight and stretched out, then it cannot be painted on to a convex form. It will be against the natural order to make a stiff branch soft and supple. Instead it can be broken in a natural way so that it follows the curve. If the object is sharply curved the motif can also be painted so that it goes almost vertically and so gets a virtually flat surface to stand on. A creeper on the other hand, such as ivy, can follow the whole way round in a natural way without any problem.

On an object curved inwards (concave), such as the inside of a bowl, the motif must in the same way fit itself into the shape. It must not curve outwards on the drawing and in that way work against the shape of the bowl, giving an impression of conflict.

Inwardly and outwardly curved leaf shapes. The leaves can be placed on china of a shape that corresponds to their shape. In a vine, for example, while you will clearly not be able to make every single leaf and flower follow the shape of the china, the general impression must be that the decoration on the china is part of the china's concave or convex form.

In other words, a leaf or something of the kind, painted on the outside of a bowl, must close in on the shape. On the other hand it must open out if it is painted on the inside. You can illustrate this using your hand. Cup it a little and, seen from the back, it is the leaf painted on the outside of the bowl. Turn it over and it represents the leaf that is going to be inside the bowl. No rule is entirely without exceptions, and this rule runs true to form, but it does give an idea of the principle of the relationship between motif and form, a question that you must give great attention to since one wrongly placed motif can ruin the whole piece. Form and motif *must* be made to agree if the result is to be successful. If you have a sheet of paper with a model on it, the paper can often be laid up against the china so that it follows its shape, and you will be able to see how the two things agree and what may have to be changed. It can also be a help to let the palm of your hand feel its way over the shape at the same time as you are looking at the model.

Principle Three

It is hard to lay down rules for positioning the motif on the china. There are countless motifs and a great number of shapes for china, so it is pointless to say, 'That is how you do it!' One or two examples will give some idea of the problem.

If you have, say, a vase, it is no good hoisting a heavy motif right up at the top. It will look as if it were threatening to slide down. On the other hand, light motif planted down at the bottom will look as if it had dropped down from higher up.

But in addition to its thickness, you must note how the motif is composed. And here you can attempt a very rough and sketchy division under the following headings:

(1) The motif is circular (e.g. a wreath)

(2) The motif can be contained within a circle (e.g. a little bunch of flowers)

(3) The motif can be composed along a vertical axis, or

(4) along a horizontal axis, that is, the motifs group

themselves along a vertical or horizontal centre-line (To help with this idea, look at the pictures on the wall. An upright picture will often be composed along a vertical axis, a tree for example, whereas a landscape picture will be composed on a horizontal line, such as the horizon itself.)

(5) The motif can be enclosed by a square, or
(6) by a triangle
(7) The motif can finally be made up of several of the foregoing possibilities combined

The round motifs (drawings 1 and 2) fit naturally into round things like dishes, plates or the bottoms of bowls. The two circles, that of the motif and that of the china, fit well together.

Motifs composed along a vertical axis can most safely be put on to china that also has a vertical axis in its line. Slender vases, jars and lamps are dominated by the

vertical line, and so subjects like grasses and flowers that reach upwards fit naturally on them.

An oval dish will be dominated by the horizontal axis. You will not see the dish standing on end, but longways on and therefore the motif with the horizontal axis will be right. But if it is arranged so that it follows the short axis of the dish it may well look wrong. The less common form of motif, the oval, could also be used on an oval dish.

As for other shapes, a square motif goes well on round things since the vertical and horizontal axes of a square are the same, just as the axes of a circle are equal. Triangles have on average a stronger vertical axis and are therefore more suited to upright objects.

If the motif is made up of several of the geometric forms you must work out where the dominant form and the centre of gravity lie. Unfortunately there is not much that can be said in a general way about the many possibilities to be found here.

It should also be mentioned that branches and flowers drawn in semi-circular form will be able to follow the edge of a round plate.

Knowledge of form and colours will enable you to go against the rules and work with contrasts, but the simplest thing is to follow *Principle Three*, which runs as follows: *The weight of a motif must balance, emphasize or approach the weight of the corresponding article of china. The motif must be composed so that it harmonizes with the shape of the china.*

It must be added that a colour can displace the centre of gravity in a motif. If the centre of gravity is determined on the basis of a black-and-white drawing, and a colour is then put on one side of the motif brighter or deeper than the one put at the centre of gravity, the motif will be 'tipped up'. The classic bouquet gives us an example of this: it consists of a 'bunch' and an outlier, and if the bunch is painted in light yellows and pinks and the outlier in a deep blue, the outlier will 'weigh down' and completely upset the balance of the motif.

After these comments on geometric forms the reader

may perhaps understand the problems that abstract painters have to cope with when they are working with circles, triangles and squares!

Purely Practical

Round shapes

To get a motif properly placed on a dish or a plate it is necessary to find the centre, since the motif and the dish must have a centre in common.

If, for example, a vine is to be taken out on to the side of the dish or plate, this marking of the centre can again be useful. A semi-circle is drawn with a pair of compasses and the motif can be drawn up round it. If the dish is so big that the fully opened compasses cannot cover it, measuring paper can be used.

Measuring paper

To make measuring paper you can use a piece of writing paper which is not too broad, folded lengthwise along its axis. On the paper measurements are marked out which are likely to be wanted a number of times on the china. A piece of squared paper is excellent for the purpose, but even better is a piece of what is called millimetre paper, since it has the measurements printed on it. If it is necessary to see through the measuring paper a piece of greaseproof kitchen paper can be used, or tracing paper (architects' drawing paper).

In setting out the measurements of, say, a mug the measuring paper can be wrapped round the object – which is something you could never do with a ruler!

If the measuring paper is to be used for marking up a circle, the distance is marked off from the rim of the dish to the place where the circle is required. Now when the measuring paper is moved round the edge of the dish a line of dots can be marked off, which can be joined up afterwards with a line to produce the circle. The same process can be used with bowls. A circle can also be used if you want to lay a ground along the edge.

Oval and angular dishes

The measuring paper can be used on these too, to draw

guide-lines and mark them off.

Smaller objects

For small things like cups and candlesticks it is far easier to use your hand than measuring paper. Following the age-old method used in almost every craft, you rest one finger against the rim and hold the point of the pencil against the china at an angle so that it draws a line in the required place as you move your hand. By 'driving' the pencil round the shape in this way you can draw a fairly precise guide-line. If you find it easier, you can rotate the object (cup or candlestick) and hold the pencil still. The same method of marking can also be used on a plate or a dish.

Motifs on cups

These will normally be placed on what might be called the front side of the cup, the half of the cup that faces

A border is drawn in on a plate in the traditional crafts-man's manner, with the finger resting against the edge of the plate to maintain an even distance. You can either turn the plate round or follow the shape of the plate with your hand, whichever you find easier.

you when you are holding it in the right hand in the normal position for drinking. On drawing the motif, see p. 34.

You can use guide-lines to get the motif in the right place. Draw a line with an All Stabilo pencil from the point where the handle is joined on, down under the cup and up the other side diametrically opposite the handle. The cup is now divided into two halves, and with the aid of the measuring paper it is easy to plot the mid-point, which should be the centre or central axis of the motif. Be careful not to get a motif on a cup too high or too low. It is particularly important not to disturb the balance on a cup.

20. Fantasy Flowers and Stylized Flowers

There is a family relationship between the flowers in nature and the imaginary flowers and stylized flowers in china paintings. You might say that if the mother of the stylized flower is the living flower, its father is the fantasy flower!

Fantasy Flowers
Before you begin on stylizing it is wise to try drawing fantasy flowers. This is something that enables you to get a real feeling for the character of flowers. A fantasy flower is a hieroglyph for a real flower. Work with fantasy flowers gives both drawing practice and a feeling for flowers, so don't limit yourself to one or two attempts, but repeat them again and again. It is an excellent idea in a class, when you are waiting for the teacher's attention, to use the time for drawing practice of this kind.

Lightning sketches
You will need a sketch-block, preferably one of coarse, rough paper, and some crayons that make a strong mark (thick glass-chalk, pastel colours, ordinary wax crayons or sharpened coloured chalk). But see that they *are* crayons and not wooden coloured pencils.

Then just keep on drawing, with simple shapes, few lines, preferably in one colour but at most three or four colours, and preferably larger than life. Sketch every possible form of flower with the crayons. Try imposing a limit of 30 seconds and gradually reducing this with practice.

Don't worry if your exercises look like children's drawings! It is the basic form of the flowers that should appear, and that is just what children draw. So – draw just as it comes into your head. After a while you will be surprised to find that your flowers are both lifelike and decorative.

When you have become more expert at drawing fantasy flowers you can try replacing the crayons with watercolours or a flat brush. Do these drawings without a model or a preliminary sketch. It is also important to practice with the strokes on the tile. Try to put them together to make fantasy flowers. Keep at it. Only with constant practice will you learn to paint china.

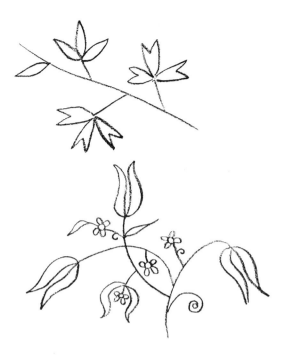

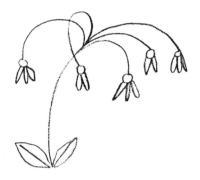

'Lightning sketches' done in 10–15 seconds. Flowers in simplified forms can be used on porcelain or delftware.

The best of the fantasy flowers can be transferred to the china as line drawings or quite simple brush drawings without the use of shading. Use strong, clear colours, and go over them a second time if necessary, but you must do it with precise, bold strokes so that the straightforward shape of the motif does not disappear.

By these means you can produce extremely decorative shapes, which are no less valid than the scrupulously brushed-in flower motifs taken from classic models.

A note though: only paint powerful-looking decorations on delftware and not on porcelain. Delftware lends itself to this form of decoration.

As a change from the 'lightning sketches' described above, try drawing a flower in one single line. The pencil or crayon must not be taken off the paper during the drawing. The best flowers can be transferred to the china. With the help of this technique, too, you can

achieve some lovely, ornamental, modern forms of decoration.

Stylized Flowers

From the colourful world of fantasy flowers it is a short step to the world of stylized flowers. The difference between the two is that the fantasy flower represents *all* flowers and no particular flower, while the stylized one is (or ought to be) a recognizable kind of flower.

This means that you must start from real life – either from a living plant or from a naturalistic sketch, a photograph in a seed catalogue or some other well-defined 'portrait' of a flower. First and foremost, you must find out what is characteristic of the flower in question and then place the emphasis on that. It may be a distinctively shaped petal, an ellipse, a jagged, circular blossom, pointed petals, a characteristic leaf

In imaginary flower done all in one line, starting just below the flower itself and finishing at the stalk. Lightning sketches and single-line drawings are not only amusing but also a source of simple and original motifs – and of personal relaxation.

A wreath of bell-flowers designed over a geometric ground-pattern. You can also draw the flower as shown in the detail drawing.

formation, a distinctive form of growth and so on.

Drawings are done without details and the same flower is drawn repeatedly, more and more simplified each time. You cannot expect to find a form that is entirely simple and yet typical straight away!

The painting of stylized flowers must be stylized as well as the drawing. And that means that there must be only 'symbolic' shading. The shadows must not be naturalistic, or the flower will be 'at odds with itself'.

Stylized wreath of bell-flowers

The floral wreath illustrated below left is an example of how an exercise in stylization can be performed. It is built on the foundation of a bell-flower, which is simple and easy to stylize.

The flower was first drawn and simplified several times on paper until it took its final form. The immediate idea was to use the flowers in a wreath. Two circles were therefore drawn with the same centre but different radii. The circumferences were then divided by means of four diagonals, which were extended beyond the circumferences. They appear in dotted lines on the drawing. Incidentally it is a help to draw on a piece of circle-paper.

Using the diameters as centre-lines, the bell-flowers can now be drawn in. To make a wreath out of them, however, the heads of the flowers must be linked together.

A new circle was drawn outside the others and curves were drawn freehand from the bottom of the flowers to the point where the outside circle is cut by a diagonal. These curves, which themselves give the motif an effect of flowers, made it hang together, but there was still something missing – a finishing touch to the heads of the flowers, to give the feeling that a bell-flower is something more than just a head.

Stylized leaves were then added, making use of the connecting curves between the flowers. Note that in the drawing use is made both of the diagonals and of the intersection between the curves that were drawn to the outside circle.

Once the motif has been drawn all the guide-lines can

be rubbed out. The inside circle remains, as it were to carry the whole wreath – it is rubbed out only where it is broken by the leaves.

The extra head shows how the bell-flowers can look if they are drawn more closed, and how you can brighten up the chain further with simple lines if you want to. The wreath drawn here can be used as a motif for a ground. For the stylizing of similar borders, graph tracing paper is recommended, or loose-leaf squared paper.

A simple, timeless leaf design, suitable for use with a ground. The motif can be drawn along the diagonals of a tile.

21. Laying a Ground

To tint the surface of a piece of china by padding paint over it is called laying a ground – or laying a *fond*; the French word comes from the Latin *fundus*, meaning a base or ground.

The surface of a white piece of china is normally cool and smooth in its whiteness, but it receives a play of colour from light and shade, which can give it a warm glow or a more bluish, chilly gleam. A piece of pottery has a more 'live' surface, and even after the clay has been glazed it retains the quality of its material – its body, as potters say. If you lay a ground on china it seldom gains in texture – on the contrary, it loses its characteristic porcelain surface. Grounds should therefore be approached with care. Not all china will be the better for a ground. It would be a shame to rob a fine piece of porcelain of its distinctive whiteness, and to make a thin, precious porcelain bowl, which is very nearly transparent, heavy and ugly. But gradually, as you work with china, you will learn to know its nature, and there will no longer be any doubt about when you should allow yourself to use a ground. Here, as with all china painting, our most important commandment applies: respect the special qualities of china and china paints! Delftware, with its strength and solidity, will often be better suited to a ground.

If you lay a ground, it will not be just for the sake of the ground itself but also for the motif that is to appear on the ground; here too there are questions that must be considered.

Drawing the Motif
For our experiment with ground-laying we have chosen a tile, which no one could call a particularly distinguished piece of china! As a motif we shall draw one of these little classic figures.

Start by drawing the motif, placing it in the middle of the tile. You can find the middle quite easily by drawing the two diagonals from corner to corner. Do not make the motif either too big or too small: if it is too big it will cease to be a decoration and become a drawing, and if it is too small it will be lost on the surface. By using the diagonals as guide-lines a square can be drawn to surround the motif and to help with the drawing. The motif is first drawn with a pen, with the lines not too thin. Use a black paint mixed with sugar.

Laying the Ground

For the ground-laying itself, if you are working on relatively large surfaces it is a good idea to have a grounding brush to spread the paint with, and a little piece of foam rubber with 'skin' on. (See the list of materials on p. 70.)

All china paints can be used for ground-laying,

The paint is padded over the surface of the china with foam-rubber. On the left, a completed tile with a narrow border and a drawn leaf-design.

though they are not all equally easy to work with. Here we have chosen one of the easier colours. Avoid blue, especially dark blue, in your first attempts; it is coarse-grained and therefore hard to pad on smoothly.

China paints are translucent, so when a colour is padded on it will be thinner and more transparent than if it had been painted on. You will not therefore obscure the drawn motif or make the line any fainter even if you pad over it several times. The longer the paint is padded the lighter it becomes.

For the ground, you mix:
10mm. grass green
plus half that amount of copaiba balsam (no turpentine!)
plus $\frac{1}{10}$ the amount of flux

The grounding paint must be mixed for at least 6 minutes. The more work you put into the grinding, the more beautiful the ground surface will become. Finally, add 2 drops of copaiba balsam, since a grounding paint must be more oily than a colour used for painting.

Put the ready-ground heap of paint on to the tile on which the ground is to be laid with a spatula or grounding brush. Spread the paint over the surface with the spatula or grounding brush. Now bend the foam rubber over your index finger, holding it in place with your thumb and third finger. Put a couple of drops of copaiba balsam on the corner of the mixing-tile – use the plastic handle of the brush to drip it on with. Dip the foam rubber in this, and then begin to pad the paint smoothly over the tile.

Working with copaiba balsam, you can allow yourself 10–12 minutes for the work; not only will the ground dry so that the padding becomes uneven, but also, as mentioned before, the colour gets lighter and lighter the longer it is padded. It will be better for the ground to look too light than too dark. An oily grounding paint will give a light colour, while a really dry paint will come out darker.

If you find it difficult to make the ground join up, dip the foam rubber into the oil on the mixing-tile now and then.

Start padding in the top left-hand corner of the tile

and work towards the right. When you have covered the whole surface horizontally, go on to pad from the top downwards, so that the surface will be padded both horizontally and vertically. When the surface is entirely covered with the grounding paint pad it quite lightly, changing direction the whole time.

As soon as the ground is smooth it is finished, and can be put aside to dry in preparation for firing. The tile should dry for an hour on the radiator, completely covered, since the ground very quickly attracts dust. If you have a curved dish or bowl at hand it is a good idea to lay that over it.

When the padding is finished the foam rubber must be thrown away, as it cannot be cleaned. Luckily, it is quite cheap.

Flux
The flux added to the grounding colour has the effect of making the ground shiny. Flux can be added to any ground, and *must* be added to blue paints to ensure the best results. If you want a matt ground you can leave out the flux, but even then it is not certain that the ground will not become shiny in the firing; it can be a bit of a gamble. In any case, all china paints contain some flux. To get a matt ground the use of matt colours is a good idea. (See p. 87.)

Copies of a set of classic leaf designs.

Use of a Silk Pad
The use of a silk pad is certainly more usual than padding with foam rubber, but practical trials have shown that with foam rubber beginners can very quickly manage to pad on a completely smooth ground, which is by no means always so easy with silk. On the other hand, when paints are used that have been ground with turpentine you cannot use foam rubber, since the turpentine attacks the rubber and makes it crumble.

The silk pad is made of pure silk (or the nearest thing available if pure silk is not to be had). The silk is cut into pieces about 7cm. (3in.) square. Cut several different sizes while you are about it, for larger or smaller jobs. Place the silk double over balls of cotton wool. (Since the pad has to be elastic, the cellulose substitute cannot be used.) Then fasten the silk loosely round the cotton wool with an elastic band. A silk pad can be washed out in spirit and soapy water and used again after the cotton wool has been removed.

Shading on Ground Motifs
If you want to shade a motif standing on a ground, it has to be done after the ground has completely dried. It is helpful to lay a piece of tissue-paper over the lower part of the work while you are shading, so that you will not put your hand on the ground. You can also fire the work before shading, so as to be quite sure that the ground will not be damaged.

Motifs in Other Colours
So far we have drawn only the outlines of the motif in black on the painted work and then laid the ground, so that the motif itself has taken on the colour of the ground. If you want to paint the motif in some colour other than that of the ground, wash away the ground from the pattern of the lines while it is still wet. This can be done with dry cotton wool rolled round a brush handle. It is possible to do this very precisely, but if any of the grounding paint still remains it can be removed when the ground is dry, using the etching pen and a cloth dipped in alcohol or a brush moistened with turpentine.

Padding of Borders

If you want to pad a border on a cylindrical mug or vase you can cover it with Sellotape or other adhesive tape (brown gummed paper will not do) up to the point at which the padded edge is to go. In that way you avoid dabbing on paint where there should not be any, and you get a razor-sharp edge to the ground when the tape is removed. The tape can also be used on a tile when you want to leave a narrow white edge of china all round, which looks very pretty. The tape is taken off while the ground is still wet. A larger pattern can be padded on to a surface using a stencil cut from paper, such as brown wrapping paper. The paper is fixed to the china with a piece of double-sided tape, which is stuck on between the subject and the paper. Pad through the holes in the stencil and the paper can be removed at once and used again. You will get the best effects if the stencil is cut simple and large.

Laying a Ground

It is practical (and quiet) to lay a foam rubber underlay about 30cm. × 40cm. (12in. × 16in.) under the work when you are padding. Such an underlay can be bought for a few pence at the soap counter of department stores.

In working on grounds in class it is advisable to start the work at the beginning of a period, since it is impossible to move a wet subject without destroying it. If the least damage should occur you must wash the ground off and begin again, as it is not possible to make corrections.

If the drawing does not look quite right you can go over the line after the ground is laid, using a brush and paint ground in the usual way.

Single specks of fluff and other foreign bodies on a wet ground can be removed with a dry corner of the piece of foam rubber used for padding on the paint, or with the drawing pen.

It is advisable not to pad in a room with a carpet, as the dust will rise if anyone walks across the floor – even if it has just been hoovered. A kitchen is the best place to pad, as that is where there will be the least dust.

22. Spirit Ground

What has been said in the foregoing chapter about ground-laying is generally true of the spirit ground as well. Here, too, care should be taken. It is a slightly risky technique, which needs to be used with great moderation and a marked aesthetic sense. Both technically and artistically a spirit ground often has more of an amateurish look about it than it ought to.

With this warning in mind, let us go on to the spirit ground.

Among materials that we have not used before we have to use a sponge – an ordinary old-fashioned natural sponge, which can be bought at an artists' supplier's or craft shop. The sponge can be cut up into several pieces.

Drawing the Motif

We shall use a tile again for this exercise, and if you want to use the hazelnut as a motif (see p. 82), you must once again ensure that the motif is placed in the middle of the tile by drawing diagonals. The centre of the motif must be at the point of intersection.

When the pencil drawing is ready it is drawn in with pen, using violet ground with sugar.

Laying the Ground

For the grounding colour, grind:
10mm. ($\frac{3}{8}$in.) dark yellow
    plus half as much copaiba balsam as there is paint
    And in a separate heap, grind:
4mm. ($\frac{1}{8}$in.) violet
    plus half as much copaiba balsam
Instead of the chestnut brown you can use sepia brown. The sepia brown will give a softer tone.

Put the yellow paint on to the tile and pad it out over the whole surface with the piece of foam rubber as

The hazelnut motif drawn in brown tones in a spirit ground. The marbled spirit ground technique cannot always be harmonized with the present-day preference for clear, simple colour decorations. Frames for titles like these can be obtained in various sizes.

described in the previous chapter. While the yellow paint is still fluid, pad the brown grounding paint lightly (with the same piece of foam rubber if necessary) over the yellow in the corners and along the edges. Don't go too far in.

The ground must now be left for a moment until it has set; meanwhile prepare a spirit mixture consisting of:

    1 part water
    2 parts alcohol

Moisten the sponge in this mixture and pad gently round the motif from the inside outwards. (Avoid the sugar drawing.) When the surface of the ground comes in contact with the spirit mixture the two combine and form a sort of marbling.

The work with the ground is now finished and it is left to dry for about an hour.

Shading

We can here consider the ground as an undercoat for the motif and we can shade on top of it.

First shading

If there is some of the chestnut brown paint left over grind it with turpentine. If the sepia brown colour has been used, the shading can be done with that.

Second shading

Use the same colour for this, with the addition of a trace of black.

If you want to paint the motif in natural colour, wash it out as described in the previous chapter.

An old Imperial Japanese coat of arms, originally in grey tones. Such a timeless motif is well adapted to use with a spirit ground; you can imagine the grey areas behind the motif growing darker towards the edges. The relative sizes of the tile and the leaf motif should be roughly the same as those of the hazelnut and the tile in the previous illustration.

Motif Without Drawn Outlines

If you prefer the motif without an enclosing outline such as a pen drawing gives, you can use an Indian ink drawing, which disappears in firing. (See p. 36.) Remember to brush in those places where the outline is to be emphasized.

Firing

The tile is now ready for firing. It needs no cleaning, since the whole tile is painted, but remember to examine the back of it and mark it with your name if you are sharing a kiln with others.

After firing the tile can be used as a plate for hot dishes or other objects.

The Sponge

The sponge can be cleaned with spirit and water and used over and over again. Other kinds of sponges can be used instead of the natural sponge but they will often make the surface look spotted or patterned in some other way. It will be a matter of taste whether you like it or not.

23. Running Ground

The technique of the running ground is extremely simple and its use can produce some quite decorative effects. Like the other grounding processes it is important to use it with discretion, and since the china more or less 'disappears' under the running ground, you should not waste good or expensive china on what may turn out to be no more than an experiment.

The running ground should not be laid on delicately formed objects, since the process is itself rather a crude one. Finely shaped cups, for instance, will easily be 'crushed' by a running ground. The irregular colour patterns will conceal the true shape.

If you just want to see what a running ground looks

Running ground on beakers. On one of them the rim has been covered with plastic tape so that the china retains its own colour. In using this technique it is important that the colours should harmonize.

like, or to experiment with different colours, you can use a tile – you will be able to wash it off afterwards – or else you can use a little vase.

Grind the chosen colours with oil and turpentine, using a little more oil than usual and a little less turpentine, together with flux. (See p. 80.)

The colours are applied so that they do not completely cover the object, perhaps in stripes or in 'blobs'.

As soon as the colours are painted on clean the brush and dip it in turpentine. Hold the vase upside down, at an angle, and squeeze the turpentine from the brush out against the edge of the base of the vase so that it runs down over the paint and makes a pattern. Repeat this all the way round, moving the brush along the edge. The work should be finished in about 8 minutes, otherwise the paint will get too dry and will not be carried down with the turpentine. Admittedly this technique is largely a matter of luck, but it is included here because it gives a good opportunity for practice in matching colours.

24. Negative Line Drawing on a Ground

A negative line drawing on a ground means a motif in white on a dark ground. The motif is scraped or scratched in the ground so that it appears in the colour of the china. A dark ground is most suitable for this, and instructions are given here for a method of laying a ground that, no matter what colour is used, will give a darker result than the method described earlier.

For the snowflake motif (see p. 85), which we may think of as decoration for a tile or a little round coaster, a blue or dark green will be suitable: cool colours should be used with snow. Dark blue and dark green paints, like violets, are difficult to grind smoothly. Here is a chance for you to practise! Even if you grind longer than for the other grounding colours you may still not be able to get an absolutely smooth ground. But you will get a more lively surface, which nowadays will often be preferred to the even, 'perfect' and consequently heavier grounds one came across in the old days, which could look a bit cold. But that is not to say that you should not take trouble with your grounds. For the preparation of all grounds, but most of all for the coarse-grained ones, a glass muller is recommended – a 'glass-drop' with a flat bottom.

Laying a Dark Ground

For this exercise, let us suppose we are using the snowflake motif on a little round china coaster for a glass (about 6cm. or 2in. across). The mixture of colours given below will be appropriate; if you want to use the motif on a tile you will need twice as much paint. For the blue ground, grind:

about 12mm. ($\frac{1}{2}$in.) blue

plus $\frac{1}{10}$ flux plus oil

Put half the mixed paint on the china. The half remaining on the mixing tile must be protected from dust.

Pad the ground smoothly as described before. When the padding is finished the china must not be touched for another 16–18 minutes.

If you feel that the paint has been ground too oily you must let it stand five minutes longer, or there is a danger that it will lift during the next process. If that happens you will generally have to start all over again.

When the 16–18 minutes are up pad the ground again (in the interval you might well be doing some drawing practice); if the old pad is worn out take a new one. The padding must be done gently on the surface of the first ground using the rest of the paint on the mixing tile, which you will have ground in advance. Continue with the padding until the ground is completely smooth all over, which generally happens pretty quickly. However, you must not go on too long; padding for too long may result in the lower coat of paint lifting.

Dark coloured grounds, in contrast to light ones, give an almost opaque surface when padded twice. (Only black gives a completely opaque result.)

Drawing the Motif

After an hour the paint will be dry enough for the motif to be drawn on it with an ordinary pencil. The line must be very light, even though it will disappear in firing. If you find it hard to draw the motif freehand directly on the ground, it can be transferred by means of the hatching method. (See p. 41.) But instead of hatching with a pencil, you use white chalk, or possibly one of those white pencils used for manicure and sold in chemists' shops or department stores. A pencil transfer will not be seen very clearly.

The outline is scraped out with an etching pen. This is what produces the negative effect; the white colour of the porcelain stands out and shows the pattern. Go over the work a second time to get the line as correct and precise as possible. In most cases a line $\frac{1}{2}$mm.–1mm. (about $\frac{1}{8}$in.) wide will be right. A white line on a black ground always looks broader than it really is. (See p. 33.)

It is best to scrape the line in the ground as soon as the paint is dry. That way you do not run the risk that the paint will come off unevenly, which can happen if

The motif is drawn with the aid of a circle-divider (see p. 42) and scraped out with the etching pen.

it is left too long, and the work becomes generally simpler. If you don't have time to do the scraping work the day that the ground is laid, it will be advisable to use a finer etching pen.

Ground-laying oil is recommended for negative drawing, since it does not lift so easily during scraping.

Initials on a ground

If you want initials or some other form of signature inlaid in the ground you can do the first drawing with Indian ink before the ground is laid and then take it out by scraping. That method cannot be used, however, if the ground is completely opaque, but then you can use one of the methods of cleaning described earlier. (On initials, see also p. 25.)

Removing the Ground from Borders

A white rim or border on china is always effective, because the white china is allowed to play its part.

The rim – or the border on a cup, which should also be decorated with a pattern – is covered with Sellotape, which can be taken off when the ground has been laid. If you prefer you can wait until the paint is dry. (See the jug on p. 99.)

If you want to put on a gold edge (fillet) or draw a border outside the ground, for instance on a plate or dish, the ground must again be removed. You do this with your thumb, which you put into a dry cloth and wipe round the wet edge of the ground once or more, to the required width. Support it with your index finger underneath the edge of the plate or dish.

If the ground paint has dried the cloth will first have to be moistened with turpentine and then cleaned with cellulose thinner; that way it will not make stains on the china, and the china will be ready for the gold to be put on. An intermediate firing is recommended.

25. Reserving Areas in a Ground

Coloured Motif in a Ground

Using this method you can reserve an area for a motif that you want to enclose in a ground. For beginners these will be fairly small motifs with a not too difficult outline, since the work can be rather dull if the motif is complicated.

When the ground has been laid and has dried for about an hour, draw the outline of the motif lightly in pencil or transfer it with chalk as described on p. 85. Scrape the outline out with the etching pen as a boundary on the surrounding ground, so that it does not get damaged in the subsequent cleaning. The remaining ground paint inside the boundary is taken off with a razor blade (you can get special handles with grooves for fixing a bit of razor blade). Any paint still remaining is cleaned off with cotton wool moistened in turpentine and rolled on to the brush-handle. For larger areas you can use a finger in a damp cloth, but in that case be careful of the outlines. The etched line is helpful here.

The motif can now be drawn and painted in the usual way. An intermediate firing is recommended, however; if you want to avoid that, lay a piece of tissue paper over the ground so that it does not get spoiled during the drawing and painting. There will be no way of repairing it if it does.

Another Method

The motif can also be drawn before you lay the ground, after which it is fired and the ground is laid. Any places where the ground comes in over the motif are cleaned off while it is still wet with a little dry cotton wool rolled round the brush-handle, or with a finger in a dry cloth.

With care, a light-coloured ground can be laid round a dark motif without an intermediate firing.

26. Powder Ground

The kind of ground that gives the deepest tone that can be obtained on china is called powder ground. The surface of the colour is very uniform and completely opaque when dark colours are used, so in using powder ground you must consider whether you want at the same time to preserve the character of the china. If you do, you may well have to be content with a partial covering of the surface.

The technique is used particularly by the famous French porcelain factory of Sèvres, which was founded in 1738 and has become the leading centre for the art of porcelain in Europe.

All china paints can be used for powder grounds. Specially to be recommended is the 'matt colour assortment' which can be obtained in eleven different shades in the most generally used colours. These paints can be used for all kinds of ground and china painting in which a matt surface is desired.

Powder ground is laid in two stages. First an ordinary ground, such as is described on p. 79, but with the paint mixed in slightly different proportions, then the actual 'powdering'. Both parts are done with the same paint.

Applying the Ground

Work with powder ground makes a good deal of dust, so it will be a good idea to put a big piece of paper over the underlay before you begin. The paper can be thrown away when the job is finished.

To the basic ground (see p. 79) you add a few extra drops of thick oil to hold the powder on the paint. The ground is padded on smoothly and then must be left untouched for about 6 minutes.

While you are waiting you can get ready for the powdering. Gently roll up a little ball of cotton wool,

and as described earlier breathe or blow on it so that it will not cause fluff.

The same powder paint is used for the powdering as was used for laying the ground. The powder is poured out straight from the glass tube on to a piece of grease-proof paper. As a rough guide, allow a little more than you used for the ground-laying. There will thus be quite a lot of powder in this ground, but unfortunately it is impossible to give any precise quantity.

When the 6 minutes are up, dip the cotton wool in the dry powder and sprinkle the powder over the surface of the ground, which is still wet and so must not be touched too much by the cotton wool. When the powder in the cotton wool runs out the cotton wool is simply dipped in the dry powder, and you go on in that way until the surface of the ground looks like a piece of velvet. If you run out of powder paint shake a little more out on to the paper, but not too much at a time, since any left over cannot be put back in the tube as it may have become dirty. Leftover paint may on the other hand be wrapped up in the greaseproof paper for further ground-laying with the same colour. If you do that, put the name of the paint on the paper for later on.

The powder paint must be left on the ground until it sticks to it. That will take about 10 minutes. You can then brush off the excess powder with cotton wool – if you like, the same ball of cotton wool you used for powdering. Simply brush off the loose powder paint on the china on to the paper you put over the underlay and throw it away.

Drawing a Motif on the Ground

For the first powder ground we have chosen a simple little motif, which can be drawn freehand with the brush-handle in the wet ground. It must be said at once that it is almost impossible to make corrections in the ground, and the drawing must therefore be executed with considerable firmness. When the job has been left to dry for the usual hour, however, you will be able to go over the first lines with the etching pen and scrape the paint away from the white parts. It is advisable to draw the motif several times on paper to get it just right before you draw it properly on the ground.

If you like you can pick out the motif in gold, but if you do so you will need an intermediate firing before the gold is applied. (See p. 109.)

Motif Inlaid on Powder Ground
Any motifs can be inlaid on a powder ground in the same way as was described on p. 86. When the ground is thoroughly dry it will be possible for the motif to be transferred by means of the hatching method with chalk. It will be best, however, to remove the larger bits with a razor blade, since a damp cloth will easily destroy the powder ground.

Powder Ground
On a decorated plate with a rim (the rim is the outer, broad edge, the flat surface being called the plate) you can paint a motif in the middle of the plate and lay a powder ground on the standard.

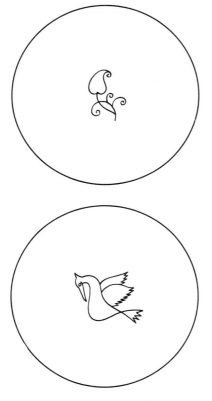

Two old decorative ornaments which fully meet the contemporary desire for simplicity.

27. Landscape Painting

The Landscape on a Flat Surface

If you want to paint landscapes on porcelain you should look for subjects that do not have a real perspective but rather a kind of 'scenic effect'. You have only to look at the work of the old Dutch tile painters to understand this. There is very seldom any perspective in their decorations; the motifs are as it were built up on a horizontal line on which the elements of the picture are artistically arranged, a bit like actors and properties on a shallow stage, with no back-cloth!

There are two main principles to follow in positioning and shaping of landscape motifs. You can contain the motif within a circle or a square, which will hold it together, and build it up so that the square or the circle is filled out in a natural, harmonious way. Or you can have a landscape without beginning or end – that is, you can let it appear evenly all over the china so that the white colour of the china plays its part as an important element of the picture. Again we come back to an important point: the motif must look as if it had been 'breathed' on to the surface.

Too strong an effect of perspective can in some cases be avoided by setting the picture in a frame.

Drawing and Padding

It is an advantage for beginners to do a preliminary sketch with sugar paint (see p. 34), but the drawing must be very light. In real life things have no outlines at all – it is the different colours that make them stand out from one another – but the sketch gives you a certain grasp of the work and is particularly valuable when there are large connected areas that have to be padded, such as water, sky or earth. Remember that clouds never have outlines.

You do the padding as shown on p. 80, then after

Cream-pot with a landscape motif. The cream-pot is part of a porcelain breakfast set decorated with polychrome motifs. Made in the Royal Danish Porcelain Factory, about 1780–1800. The complete breakfast set is on display at the Art Industry Museum, Copenhagen.

drying the motif can be shaded down in the darker colours and shadows.

If there are changes of colour that have to be blurred, leave a bit of white china between the two colours like a stripe. Then you can blend the colours together with a clean pad, if necessary using a little pure oil. The outer colours of a landscape can be faded out into the white china in the same way.

If a ground has to change over from very dark shades to light tones, put on plenty of the ground paint in the darkest parts and only a little in the light parts, and then pad – finishing with pure oil.

Faint Background

The process described above can be reversed in the

E

case of a light, distant background, by first painting the motif completely, letting it dry and then carefully padding in the background towards the motif. The background can also be painted on with ordinary paints and brush, using light strokes.

Choose the method that suits the subject best.

A light ground can be carefully padded in to a dark motif, once it is dry. With a darker ground it is best to use an intermediate firing before it is laid.

A faint background can also be used for other kinds of painting, such as flowers, birds, animals and so on.

A Landscape without Outlines

If you want a landscape without outlines, with only the colours as dividing lines, you can use an All Stabilo pencil, whose marks disappear in the firing. With care you can pad and paint lightly over it, unlike a pencil drawing, which completely disappears when it comes into contact with china paints.

After the sketch is made the light colours are ground first and can be padded on or, for a little motif, painted on. After that you go on with the darker colours and shadows. Finally go over the outline again.

Be careful that the Stabilo pencil's outline does not cheat you so that there is something missing in the motif after firing. Brush over again in the right places.

Landscapes Using the Berlin Technique

The experienced china painter who can work by himself will be able to paint and shade a landscape completely without intermediate firing by using the Berlin technique. (See p. 45.)

Ground-Laying Oil

This is the most expensive oil used in china painting. It is highly recommended if you have mastered the Berlin technique. The oil is ground up with powder colours just like other oils, but without the addition of turpentine, or with only very little turpentine. Aniseed oil is added for big jobs.

This oil is especially suitable when you are working without intermediate firing and a motif is completely painted without a break in the work. Using this oil you can apply the paint lightly and thinly, to very fine effect. There is nothing to worry about if the motif looks too pale after firing: a further shading on the pale background will make the whole even finer.

If you want to use ground-laying oil when you are working with the Meissen technique (see p. 45) without intermediate firing, allow the undercoat to set for 6–8 minutes, after which the paint is receptive and the shading can be lightly brushed on to the undercoat.

If ground-laying oil is used for china painting with intermediate firing it will not stand further shading.

28. Leaf Exercises

For beginners in china painting – and for that matter for the more advanced student – leaves can present difficulties. One trouble is that students are apt to reduce them to 'a patch of green', a mere accessory to the flowers; another is that they are often shaded quite haphazardly, with no regard for the original.

Shading calls for good powers of observation combined with logic. How are the shadows made, what casts a shadow on what, does the leaf stick straight out or hang down or stand upright? It is impossible to give firm rules; it all depends on the shifting light.

Gardeners talk of full shadow, half shadow and light. We can work with the same ideas once we are clear how light falls. It is best if you draw leaves directly from nature, without picking them and taking them indoors, where you depend on light from a window or on artificial light. So take your sketch-block out into the garden or into a wood.

The sketches reproduced on pp. 91–92 are intended as basic exercises if you cannot manage to paint out of doors. First copy the leaves on paper and put in the shadows by shading with pencil. You can also copy the leaves on to tiles for practice. Many leaves, with their beautiful and varied shapes, can be the subjects of separate motifs.

Vetch leaves (left). The stalk stands upright and the light falls on the leaves from above. The leaves standing up on each side of the stalk are in shadow, while the leaves lying down next to them are lit. Shadows appear where the leaves are folded along the central rib. The small sketches show details of the vetch leaves.

The three tender young dandelion leaves, (right), are shown after the first shading (below) and after the second shading (above). The sun is supposed to be shining on them obliquely, from above left. The leaf on the left therefore only gets a shadow from its own folds. It shades the centre leaf, which gets a powerful shadow at the bottom; the shadow at the top of it appears only as a result of the fold in the leaf. The right-hand leaf gets a shadow from the centre leaf, strongest where the two leaves are closest together.

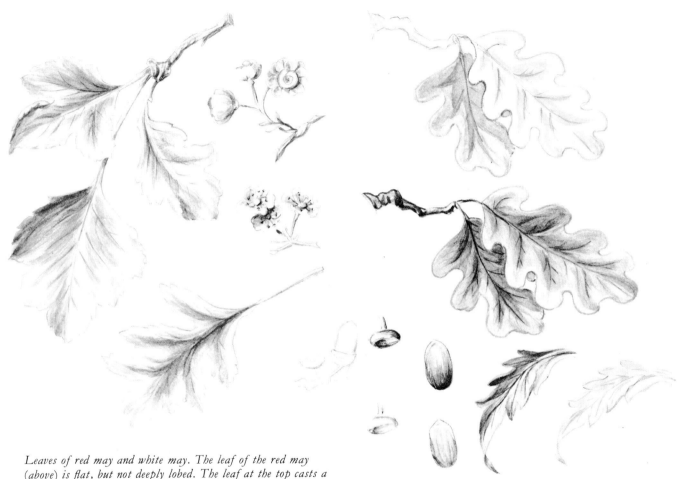

Leaves of red may and white may. The leaf of the red may (above) is flat, but not deeply lobed. The leaf at the top casts a shadow on the one below it, and also on itself where it is bent over. The leaf on the right bends back slightly so that you can see a bit of its underside. The shadows bring out the slight curve of the leaf and the bright patch along the central rib. The white may leaves (below) are quite flat, so there will be no great contrasts of light and shade. The shadows lie on the side-ribs and in towards the centre, and emphasize the shape of the leaf. Beside the leaves, flowers of the red may (above) and the white may (below).

Two oak leaves after the first and second shadings. Oak leaves often curve away from one another along the central rib, as they do here. The leaves are seen from above. The upper leaf casts a heavy shadow on the lower. The upper is strongly lit and presents a bright contrast to the lower. The detail drawings show acorns and the little 'cup' that the acorns grow in.

Below, drooping poppy leaves, also in two shadings. Note how the points of the leaves curl up.

92

29. Fruit

As an example of fruit painting we have chosen an apple; at the end of the section we shall have a look at various other fruits. It will be wisest to make the first attempts at painting them on a white tile before moving on to bigger things.

For our next exercise let us think of an apple, which is yellow, greenish and red. With an All Stabilo pencil, draw an apple like the one above, with leaf and stalk.

For each of these grind the following colours with copaiba balsam:

3mm. ($\frac{1}{8}$in.) dark yellow
3mm. ($\frac{1}{8}$in.) light green
3mm. ($\frac{1}{8}$in.) scarlet

No turpentine is used for this exercise, or at any rate very little; that makes it easier for you to start shading right away as soon as the paint is set. The job is not intended to be fired.

If you have mastered the Berlin technique you can use turpentine in later exercises. You will be able to apply the paint thinner and more lightly.

The Undercoat

When you are painting large fruit like apples and pears it is best to use a large brush. Big brushes will always give the smoothest results on big surfaces.

The paints are put on with strokes that follow the shape of the apple. Begin with the yellow, painting it in the middle of the apple. Apply the two other colours outwards towards the outline of the apple. Let the green dominate round the leaf and the red in the direction of the stalk. Leave a strip of white china uncovered between the three colours. Clean the brush, and with a little oil paint the colours together in a blurred transition. A pad or your finger can also be used.

Shading

The shading takes place immediately after. Grind:

yellow undercoat plus $\frac{1}{2}$mm. orange
green plus $\frac{1}{2}$mm. dark green plus a little black
1mm. dark red for shading the red.

Shade half way up the first undercoat, as shown above. Shape the strokes so that the apple is rounded out. The second shading should be laid halfway in over the first.

The stalk is shaded with violet.

The leaf is shaded with the green paint plus a little black.

Painting Fruit

You ought to draw several apples and colour them before you finally venture to paint an apple on china. Draw from life and try different kinds of apples – there are countless apples in a variety of shapes and with their colours in stripes or patches. When you are painting apples of those kinds, do not put the stripes and patches on until the second shading.

If you are an experienced china painter, you can use the grounding oil mentioned in the previous chapter, which is best suited for the Berlin technique, but other oils are perfectly acceptable. If you use this technique all the colours in the apple must be ground beforehand and gently worked into one another. Start with the lightest colours and finish with the darkest – that will usually give the most natural result. As you will remember, the motif is painted completely without intermediate firing when the Berlin technique is used.

If the motifs are very big it will be wise to add a trace of aniseed oil in grinding the paints so that they will stay fluid.

In choosing china to paint fruit on, remember that the size of the motif depends on the size of the china. A plate may look too heavy and strong if the motif – especially heavy apples and pears – is too big.

Apples and pears, which are highly three-dimensional in form if painted naturalistically, will in most cases look best on flat objects. If they are painted on very curved pieces you may get a conflict between the shape and the motif. Try stylized fruit motifs, where the colour merely hints at the shape rather than rounding things out. (For leaves, see pp. 91–92.)

Other Fruit

Pears

The first coat on a green or grey pear can be of the lightest colour, or the two lightest colours, that the pear has. After that, shade down in the darkest tones so as to reveal the oval or round shape of the pear. Red-brown pears are painted in the same way as apples. Suggestion for colours: yellow-green plus a little brown, grass-green plus a little brown. Add a little black for shading.

Plums, Grapes, etc.

These fruits, which have a smooth and shiny skin, generally have a shiny, reflecting spot which should really be included in the painting to give life to the fruit. You can do that by using a light colour on the spot in question. Remember that the light comes only from one angle: the spot on all the grapes or plums will therefore lie on the light side and the dark shadows will be on the opposite side, unless leaves or branches are also casting shadows.

Use the lightest colour of all for the first coat, which will remain on the bright spot, but will be shaded over elsewhere. If you are painting from life you will need to make sure that the light falls so that the fruits get their bright spot on one side, on either the upper or the lower half of the fruit.

Hips

The hip and similar firm fruits of red colour are first given a thin undercoat of scarlet. The first shading is done with the same colour, and the second with dark red. If you want a clearly marked outline you can finish with a touch of chestnut brown mixed with the shading colour where the fruit is rounded out towards the stalk. Note that the colour of the hip can be anything from light orange to deep red.

Raspberries and Blackberries

Draw the outline as a grey pen sketch (perhaps with icing sugar). The little clusters of fruit that make up raspberries and blackberries are drawn as small rings or circles; you should not put in as many as there are in real life or they will look unnatural.

When you have your basic drawing of a raspberry (which will not disappear in firing) you can put on a smooth coat of scarlet and shade on the dark side with dark red. Do not paint the small circles with the dark red colour until the second shading; then you can give them a suggestion of shading where they are darkest. Do be careful that some of the first colour is left showing as a bright spot. To get some variety into the colour of the berries, you can do the first coat for the ripest berries in the dark red paint and shade with the same colour mixed with a tiny trace of black.

Raspberries which have a bluish gleam can be painted first with pale blue.

Blackberries are painted like raspberries. They have either a reddish or a bluish sheen, so for the undercoat you grind either

pink plus a trace of black or

pale blue

For shading, use two parts of pink to which you add one part of black. Add a little more black for the second shading so that the circles take on a really deep colour.

In painting the stalks of blackberries and raspberries the quality of the fine thorns and hairs must not be lost. They are brushed on last with a fine brush, or else you can use a pen drawing.

If the sketch drawing is done with paint containing icing sugar the hairs can be suggested at the same time as you are doing the drawing, but this must be done very lightly.

Fully ripe strawberries are painted first with scarlet and then shaded with dark red. Berries that are only half ripe are painted with scarlet on the upper half and below with a warm light green such as grass green. Shade the berry so that it becomes darker towards the bottom.

Strawberries

First draw the outline of the model with sugar paint, together with the little knobs on the fruit, but again, do not put in too many. To bring out the character of the strawberry, draw them as little V-shaped ticks.

Paint and shade smoothly.

When you have finished painting the berry and the paint is dry, the little ticks should be carefully scratched out and a yellow relief colour laid on. (For relief colours, see p. 45.) But do not let the paint be raised too high or it will come off or be worn away when the china is used.

30. The Animal Kingdom

Motifs from the animal kingdom are very popular, not least because of the opportunity they give for both naturalistic and stylized renderings. The most suitable subjects for such simplifying and dressing up in stylized form are birds and fish. You can paint them quite freely as imaginary creatures in simply drawn shapes and colour them decoratively rather than naturalistically with pure colours, which will look good on almost any china.

Game animals and birds make good subjects for shooting sets and in the same way you can use fish motifs for fishing sets (but preferably with edible fish!). Strange and rare fish from the aquarium will not be really suitable for decorating a table service – except perhaps for dessert plates – but you can use them purely for decoration. Birds, too, in a strictly naturalistic representation, will be used first and foremost for decorative purposes.

Mammals, besides the game animals mentioned above, offer great opportunities for motifs, such as children's plates with elephants and giraffes (which you may well like to do with a touch of humour), copies of prehistoric cave paintings and so on. The last-named will also be an obvious subject for treatment with a ground.

Birds from Dutch tiles in the Tonder Museum. It is both amusing and exciting to go on a hunt for old motifs, which are just as much alive today as when they were drawn.

Technique

With the introduction of animal subjects we must be careful not to lose our sense of proportion. The relative sizes must correspond with one another. To take an obvious example, an elephant will not have room to move if you put it on to a small, delicate object, and it is equally clear that a flying bird must be painted so that it gives an immediate impression of lightness and flight. Birds must be light both in colour and in brush strokes. They must not be weighed down by heavy tones, even if they are depicted sitting. It is generally true to say that animals must stand out sharply on the motif. You can therefore use a pen drawing (with sugar) as the basis of the work.

Your first coat will be in one or more light colours, according to the original colour of the animal. If the motif is to be a big one the paint can be padded on as for a ground, and then smoothed out with a brush.

For the first shading the paint is brushed lightly on to the undercoat, and not until the second shading will you put in the details. Finally, carry out any necessary brushing up and rounding out of the outlines.

If you start to concern yourself with details at too early a stage there is a danger that you will lose sight of the overall design and the work will get stuck.

With an eye to the possible introduction of sky and water into the subject, take another look at the section on landscape painting on p. 89.

For the naturalistic sketch drawing of birds (and other animals) grey paint is recommended, with perhaps a touch of dark brown added. But of course you must be sure first and foremost that you are guided by the original colour of the animal. For some animals a pure brown will be more appropriate. In drawing furry animals make sure that the outline is not sharply delineated. The fur, and the quality of it, must be visible, and the outline must not be smoothed out in the painting.

It is particularly important with animal subjects to study the original drawing most carefully before you start on the project. In many cases it will be necessary to get an extra shade of colour to be sure of producing the right result. And then, remember that it is always easiest to use the lightest shades of the original as your undercoat.

3 1. Jewelry

The use of china jewelry is a matter of fashion. In some periods you will see a lot of it, in others hardly any. The subjects are similarly dictated by fashion, and as with all other jewelry they must be made to harmonize with clothes, styles and so on.

Possibilities include small flower motifs, rococo portraits (if you care for them), abstract patterns, line ornaments and many others. But whatever you choose, remember that the art of making such ornaments, though it is classified as a 'minor' art, is a very demanding one. If a brooch looks the least bit amateurish, it disfigures more than it adorns.

Also, be careful that the ornament does not lose the quality of the china during painting, which can easily happen – it is not meant to look like enamel, horn, gold or silver, mother-of-pearl, or anything at all but china! So do not begin on jewelry until you have fully mastered the even stroke and the smooth transition in shading. It is also essential that you are able to work in a small format without losing clarity and decorative quality.

Little plates for painting can be obtained from most firing centres and in specialist shops, and pins and clips can be bought for a small sum in hobby or do-it-yourself shops, which will also stock a suitable glue.

Snowflakes (see p. 85) will fit on to the largest and second largest plates. They can be done either in positive or negative, or in gold if you like.

If you are very careful, jewelry can be given a mother-of-pearl base – the one called *iridescent lustre* is the most discreet. (For lustre, see p. 98.)

The matt china paints mentioned on p. 87 are very popular today. They can look very pretty when used for ornaments, either as a ground with a negative drawing or picked out in gold.

The hexagonal figures below have nothing to do with jewelry or with china; they are tiles from Syria and are nearly six hundred years old, but quite timeless in their simple ornamentation and figures, so that they look modern. There is wealth to be found for the china painter in ancient Islamic art – and not only for making jewelry.

Method of Working

It can be difficult to work on the small surface of an ornament, but the following method can be recommended. Thinly roll out a piece of modelling wax and stick it on a metal lid or something similar. Fasten the plate to this, which will give you the best grip on the china; if you hold the ornament in your hand it will be virtually impossible for you to reach the edges, but stuck fast in the modelling wax, the ornament can be turned round as much as you like while you are working on it.

Hexagonal Syrian tiles from about 1425. *They are about* 178mm. *(7in.) in diameter, and the originals, in the Victoria and Albert Museum in London, are carried out in blue and white. Motifs like these are quite suitable for modern ornaments.*

32. Lustre Paints

The word 'lustre' comes from the Italian *lustro,* which means 'shine'. Lustre paints are metallic oxides, which give the china a metallic shining surface.

The technique came originally from the Arab countries, where they used to cover ceramic cups and plates with a golden shining lustre. Actually they would have liked to eat and drink from pure gold – if they could afford it – but since the Koran told them that they would enjoy the good things of life on the other side, they thought they could not anticipate such joys here on earth.

You will gather from this that a lustre paint can change the character of china just as a ground can since the lustre makes the surface of the china metallic. Strictly speaking, it doesn't have much to do with china, but the effect can have a certain charm, particularly on the old jugs you often see in antique shops. These jugs are further adorned with decorative bands and stylized flowers, and this double working with lustre glazing and decoration makes it clear that you are looking at china and not metal.

The Paints

Lustre paints can be obtained in about seven colours which are all yellowish or brown in the liquid form in which they are sold. The true colour does not appear until the firing.

Lustre paints are not ready for use until the tube has been shaken. Many people prefer to use the paints straight from the tube, dipping the brush into it. If you do that you must remember to replace the cap immediately, since the paints dry very quickly. If you put the paints on to a mixing tile you can use them with a brush, but do not use too much at a time. You may

A rustic jug with lustre glaze. The jug, which is in the Danish Folk Museum in Copenhagen, is decorated with two bands of yellow ground, in one of which a motif of stylized houses and trees is painted.

find lustre thinner helpful, since it slows down the drying process. Use a horn spatula for mixing on a tile, as a metal spatula oxydizes. You must use only a drop or two of the thinner, or the metallic sheen will disappear.

A glass spatula (mentioned on p. 107) is also recommended.

Thinner can also be used when you are reaching the bottom of the tube and what is left of the paint has thickened; just add a couple of drops and shake the tube.

Putting on Lustre Paints

As with other china paints, the china must be well cleaned first; this is best done with cellulose thinner (remember that it is inflammable and dangerous to inhale), lustre thinner or naphtha. The china must not be touched with warm fingers after being cleaned. It must be at room temperature, and cannot be moved from a warmer or cooler room. If you do not follow these conditions the result will not be successful.

For a brush we recommend a short, thick brush.
Lustre paints are applied with smooth strokes.

Uneven strokes do not give the desired effect after firing, but result in several shades of colour. If necessary you can put on two coats, which will give a deeper colour. Intermediate firing is not necessary.

Clean the brushes both before and after use in one of the cleaning agents mentioned above. If larger surfaces are to be painted with lustre the paint can be padded on, using a silk pad. (See p. 80.)

A flower motif can also be painted with lustre paints and then shaded with china paints, or better still, shaded with the same lustre or with black to obtain greater depth. Intermediate firing is not strictly necessary but is recommended.

Oil of Rosemary

Lustre paints can be mixed with a drop or two of oil of rosemary. This both gives slightly lighter colours and slows down the drying process. If too much is added the paint takes on a light red tinge that is not very attractive.

Copper Lustre

Copper lustre, unlike the other lustre paints, has to be put on fairly thickly, otherwise it takes on a violet tint after firing.

Mixing Lustre Paints

Lustre paints can be mixed with one another, except for orange. You will need some practice to get good results with lustre paints, mainly because they do not always turn out the same after firing. The red lustre paint is the hardest to get right. It is advisable to put on two coats with an intermediate firing. Since lustre paints dry immediately, they only have to harden before being sent to the kiln. It is wise to mark the china before putting the lustre on.

Lustre paints must never be dried in the oven, as they shrink easily. Special care must be taken with lustre work in firing: it needs to be warmed up slowly and to be well ventilated at first, and, if it is to retain its metallic appearance, must not be put in the kiln near the element.

33. Portrait Painting

You will occasionally see portraits on old china – often of heads of state, kings and noblemen. In some cases these will have been printed, in others they are original work on the china. If you want to paint portraits in the classical style you must be quite clear that what you are doing is a pastiche; if it is to come off there must be harmony between the subject and any additional decoration, above all between the subject and the object you are painting on. You can't paint an eighteenth-century portrait on a modern teapot; you must look for a teapot of the proper period, or a pot that is so simple that it belongs to no specific period. You should never try to reproduce the style of another period until you are quite sure that you know what the things that you are trying to imitate looked like. That may sound obvious, but it is a mistake that people often make. Make use of the museums and the large number of books on the subject. Unless you are quite sure that you have the knowledge and the technical skill to attempt the task properly, you will do better not to try to reproduce period pieces. It is better to create a personal decoration, which does not pretend to be anything else, than an unsuccessful imitation. Nor is the painting of portraits in any way finer than other forms of china painting. Also, you must remember that one of the reasons why people used to paint portraits on china was that photography had not been invented!

Drawing

You can use the following mixture for the pen drawing. (It was used before for the relief colours; see p. 45.) It is very suitable for portraits, as it gives a thin outline, but it is not resistant to oil and turpentine. None the less, it is reliable for beginners. You mix:

1 part light grey

half that amount relief oil
plus turpentine for thinning

The paint should be ground up with turpentine now and then as you work.

Draw the outline and the most important details as lightly and discreetly as possible. Let the drawing dry well before starting to paint. (The drawing paint mentioned on p. 44, using aniseed oil, can be used as an alternative.)

The Undercoat

You will find it most practical to begin painting the eyes, mouth and cheeks. After that put the shadows on the face, starting with the nose, which will give the portrait its life. In some cases the shadows round the nose will be enough, but sometimes you will need to paint shadows on the china and neck and at the point where the hair meets the face. Follow the model closely. Last of all paint in the hair.

Painting and Shading

For beginners an intermediate firing is recommended before the colour of the skin and the shading is painted.

For rococo subjects we suggest the following range of colours, if the hair and eyes are brown:

eyes	violet
hair	violet plus a little black
lips	pink
cheeks	pink
shadows	blue plus black
skin	pastel pink

Not until this part of the work is finished can you paint in the skin colour. An intermediate firing is helpful, but if you are experienced you can tone in the skin colour using the Berlin technique, brushing away from the colours you have already put on. Leave a strip of white china between these and the skin colour and finally make a smooth transition with a little pure oil. If the picture looks too faint after firing you can add more paint and fire again.

Ground-laying oil can be recommended for 'wet on wet' portrait painting.

Tabatière with portraits in the lid. A tabatière is an elegantly decorated snuff-box. The one shown here, which is in the Art Industry Museum in Copenhagen, is from the Royal Danish Porcelain Factory and was painted about 1785.

In imitating rococo subjects you can use a mixture of blue and violet with the chestnut brown predominating, as caputmortuum tone (English red). This is recommended for other painting too, and also looks nice with blue predominating. It makes a good shadow-tone for rococo portraits.

Intermediate Firing

Portraits can also be painted on the same principles that we learnt at the beginning of the book – the Meissen method with an intermediate firing. In that case you put on the skin colour first and then shade down with the darker colours. You may be able to do without the intermediate firing. However, a portrait carried out by the method described above will look lighter and more delicate, and that is important in rococo subjects.

34. Tiled Tables

Many people may regard a tiled table as a difficult task, but if you proceed on the lines taught here the work should not be beyond you. There are several ways of looking at tables of this kind. Above all, of course, the size must be right, and that is what will determine the

A baroque table made of Dutch tiles painted blue. Tiled tables are the descendants of tray-tables, in which the whole top consisted of a light cup-shaped china tray with decorations. The tiled table shown above, from about 1750, is in the Kolding House Museum in Denmark.

number of tiles. If you use ordinary white tiles, the glazier can cut them. The old Dutch tiles measure 13cm. (5in.) square, which is a very attractive size. If you cannot get the glazier to cut up your tiles for you it is not hard to do it yourself. If a tile is scratched gently on the glazed side with an awl or a triangular-section file it breaks quite easily – rather like a bar of chocolate.

The next thing is to see where the table is to stand: the colours must go with the furniture, curtains and so on. Avoid round tables; square tiles can never be cut to fit really well. The unavoidable gaps or overlaps between tiles will make a horizontal or vertical pattern which conflicts with the round shape. (For tiles, see p. 20.)

The Motif

The motif – or motifs – must all be of the same style and the painting technique the same for the whole table. The motifs must not clash with one another, and there should be a natural connection and rhythm between them. Nor should the table be overcrowded – it calls for a very sure taste to make a really good job if the whole table is to be decorated. A simple row of tiles inlaid in a table can look very handsome. The more decoration there is the heavier the table will look – which means that the height and dimensions of the table must be taken into account in choosing the motif, so that all are on the same scale. A light motif will call for slender lines; a heavy one must stand on strong legs or there will be a lack of proportion. On the other hand, there is nothing to prevent you lightening a heavy piece with light decorations.

Avoid old-fashioned, heavy tables decorated with mixed spirit grounds; they are rarely attractive.

If you are copying Dutch tiles you must choose motifs that go with the smooth surface of commercial tiles; you will not get the help from the glaze that the Dutchmen got!

Avoid naturalistic landscapes with perspective – they look all wrong on the flat surface of a table.

The bigger the table, the simpler each separate motif should be; you do not want it to look like an exhibition where you move on from one tile to another to see what happens next. Also, be careful about laying grounds. If you do use a ground, let it be a light one.

If you are using flower designs, you can paint a motif on every other tile and just put a little figure in the middle of the others, or even leave them white.

Sketching, etc.

The sketch can be roughed out first on a piece of squared paper. After that it is a good idea to sketch the chosen motif full size on a big piece of paper such as architects' drawing paper. Draw in the square pattern of the tiles as well – it takes care to make a tiled table! Always be quite sure that the tiles you buy have no flaws in them. It is wise to have the board that the tiles are to lie on made at once, or you may prefer to try them out on a cardboard square of the right size. A small wooden frame should be fastened round to hold them in position. The tiles can be taken up for painting one at a time, but be careful to bear the whole design in mind.

Ground

If you want to lay a ground it will be as well to put the designs on first with sugar paint; the ground can then be padded on without intermediate firing.

For a ground you should allow 1cm. ($\frac{3}{8}$in.) powder paint per tile plus half that amount of oil. Do not use turpentine, but put a little extra oil on the mixing tile A couple of drops of aniseed oil will delay the drying.

Mounting

Tiles generally look too heavy for big trays, but a little tray can be made from two tiles and nothing else. You can also cut tiles to make them long and narrow, which can look very smart for other purposes as well as for trays. The pattern must of course follow the slender shape. Avoid round trays.

A glazier may agree to fix your tiles to the table if the joiner who does the other work cannot manage it. If you do it yourself, there are various kinds of glue on the market, and any hardware store will be able to advise you as to the best to use.

35. Changing the Size of a Model

A model is often too big or too small to go on the china. The problem can be solved at once by the use of a 'square net'. The idea is that you first lay a piece of transparent paper divided into squares over the motif. Then you draw the motif on another piece of paper with bigger or smaller squares, according to the final size of the motif, following the points where the lines of the original intersect with the lines on the square-net. The easiest, and often the most precise, way of dividing the paper into squares, if you do not want to work geometrically, is to fold it. Use tracing paper or grease-proof paper.

Measure the height or the width of the model, which-ever is greater. Mark off this measurement horizontally and vertically from the corner of the tracing paper (accurately cut out) and draw a square. Cut it out. You can confirm that it really is square by laying corner to corner. Fold the square fron side to side so that you get a square again. Fold twice more, and then open the paper out. It is now divided into 16 equal-sized squares – assuming you have done the job accurately. Go over these with the point of a pencil and place the paper over the model.

Take a new piece of paper and cut it so that it is a square whose side is the size that you want the model to be after conversion. Fold it and pencil it as before.

If the motif is very complex and hard to draw you will need a lot of squares. You can halve the squares in both directions with a ruler, or you can just fold over again. The result will be that where you previously had four squares in each direction you now have eight. If you want to you can double the number again.

By tracing the motif under the first square-net you can see exactly how the lines go and draw corresponding lines on the other squared paper.

Instead of folding the paper you could also have constructed a square-net by first marking off a horizontal line under the motif and then a vertical line to the left of it. Divide these lines into four with measuring paper. You can then complete the square-net and draw the lines to join up and across.

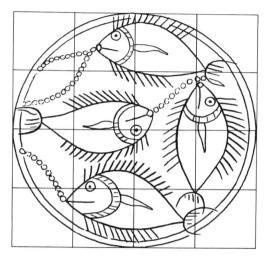

A motif is made larger or smaller with the help of a square-net. The fish motif is Egyptian and about 1500 years old. On the original the fishes are in white on a reddish background.

36. Borders and Geometric Patterns

You will often find a use for geometric patterns, for instance for borders, secondary motifs, and in conjunction with other ornamentation.

There are people who maintain that they cannot draw so much as a simple geometric pattern without an original to copy from. This can only be due to lack of self-confidence and faith in their own skill; in fact, these simple patterns and figures are remarkably easy to draw. Anyone can learn to draw motifs as simple as those shown below: it is just a matter of simple signs being repeated over and over again.

Nothing could be much simpler than these lines:

But there are considerable decorative possibilities in letters and figures, too, if they are repeated. Just look at this letter V:

And you can get an L to look like this:

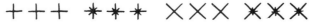

K and B can also be used:

Simple signs, such as this cross, can also be used as the basis of a pattern:

Here are several simple signs. They come to life when they are repeated:

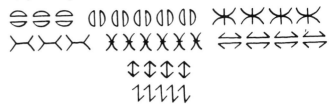

You can fix the dot to the top of an i, like this:

– and if the i gets a line to stand on it will look like this:

The last figure can also be turned upside down:

and the i's can also be drawn as garlands:

If you compose your motif along a line it gives you direction. The line will also hold the whole thing together, as in this example:

If you close up the top of a V to make a triangle, you get new possibilities:

– and two triangles and a few lines turn into leaves:

If you think of the borders illustrated in musical terms, most of them go 'dum-dum-dum-dum-dum' – a very uniform rhythm. If you want to change the beat it can be done like this: 'dum-da-dum-da-dum-da'.

Thus you can practically sing the notes of a border. There are also possibilities in rhythmic repetition. Here is another rhythm in a number of variations (try to beat them out or sing them):

The garland of i's we had just now can become a whole scale, do-re-mi and so on, and that can be sung too.

If you think these figures are too simple you can build up from them still further. The following motif began as a 7 in a 'mirror-monogram':

Then the figures acquired a hook underneath and looked like this:

– and finally a little cross-stroke to join them together.

You might have put the last stroke somewhere else:

– and finally you could have drawn the 7 as it is shown here – and you would still have several ways of varying it:

You may feel that rather softer shapes would be nicer. Well, that can be done on the same lines. But then you should turn to handwritten letters, as in this n shape:

– which is fitted out with a corresponding row underneath:

– and finally a joining line and a cross-stroke.

Now try yourself, joining perhaps a row of e's or l's, one after another. For a little variety every other one can be filled in:

Here is a row of handwritten f's. They are easy to draw freehand and make a decorative pattern. (See p. 46.)

All the figures illustrated are in a horizontal line. Of course they could also be stood on edge so that they were underneath one another (try turning the book through 90°), or turned into a secondary motif such as a circle. Entire motifs can be painted in one colour, or done in gold.

Draw two or three circles with a common centre, using compasses or the circle-paper. You need the circle in the middle only if the separate parts of the pattern have a 'middle' that has to be placed exactly. The two outside circles are the frame for the motif.

'Test dish', showing how simple geometric patterns can be built up.

To transfer the circles, and the patterns with them, to, say, a dish, you must first find the centre of the dish. Lay it upside down, with the bottom up, on a piece of paper and draw a pencil line round its circumference. Now cut out the circle you have drawn and fold it twice. When the paper is flattened out again the folds will make two diameters, and where they intersect will be the centre of the circle. Now it is easy to transfer the centre mark to the dish and mark it with a cross in pencil and the circles can be drawn.

Brushes can be fitted in the compasses instead of a pencil. If the dish is too big for a pair of compasses to be used, the marking will have to be done with measuring paper or with a cylinder divider.

Circle Motifs

A game played with pencil and compasses can also give rise to geometric patterns. On the dish at the left, it is quite clear how the circular motifs can be built up so that they grow out over the dish. To show how the motifs grow out of one another, motifs are drawn on several different dishes.

Draw several circles with the compasses, one inside the other, with varying radii so that you do not get a monotonous rhythm. Draw in two or four diameters as guide-lines. With the paper folded as it was before you got two diameters, so that the circle was divided into four. If you now fold the paper again you get eight divisions, which can be transferred to the dish. (Draw marks on the rim of the dish with the All Stabilo pencil and join them up.)

Begin with the inside circle. The four small leaves and buds in the middle follow the line of the diameters.

It is seldom much of a problem to think of designs – quite the reverse in fact, it is far more difficult to stop yourself thinking of them!

From this dish you can draw ideas and inspiration for others with a simpler look.

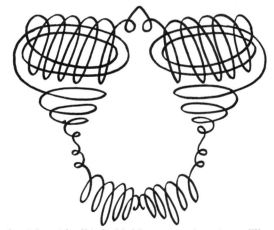

A flourish or 'doodle' doubled by means of a mirror. The effect almost of calligraphy will look well on china of a modern, matching shape.

Mirror Motifs

Several times in considering geometric patterns we have used the trick of turning the sign round so that the result is something of the nature of a mirror monogram. Quite simple flourishes ('doodles') can be turned into ornaments if they are repeated in reverse – either the whole flourish or just a part of it. You can use a little pocket mirror to help. Hold it against the flourishes at different angles. In that way you get a chance to look at the motif as a double motif with its mirror image. It is the same technique that you use when you want to make a 'corner' on the border of a piece of embroidery. It can also be used for square frame motifs on china.

37. Working with Gold

If you are sufficiently interested you can work with gold even if you are no great expert at china painting. It is a tractable material and no harder to work with than ordinary china paints.

Great, wide gold rims and overcrowded borders are not much in fashion today. Most people prefer narrow rims and light, simple borders. And for that very reason there are great possibilities, even for beginners, in painting with gold. Here is a list of the materials most used, but it must be pointed out that it is not necessary to get the whole lot right away:

Materials

China	Long, pointed flower brush
Mixing tile	Agate pencil
Glass spatula	Gold eraser
Cellulose thinner	Naphtha
Gold thinner	Fluff-free cloth and a little
Gold underlay	cotton wool
Glass brush	Relief oil
Long, oblique fillet brush	Oil of lavender

(The brushes can be obtained in various degrees of fineness. A medium size is best.)

Gold

Gold for china painting can be obtained in powder or liquid form. The liquid variety is the one most often used for instructional purposes. You can get gold paints with a smaller gold content but it pays to get only the best even if it is a bit dearer.

A glass brush consists of a little bunch of glass threads bound together. With this tool you brush the fired gold very gently, so as not to wear the surface more than necessary. This is what produces the characteristic look of gold.

Unless you are going to take up work with gold on a big scale this brush ought to be all you need. If you are going in for it in a big way you should get an agate pencil, which gives gold the deepest possible glow while being less hard on the surface than the glass brush. Agate pencils are made in several shapes, depending on what they are to be used for. They are made so that they can be used for polishing inaccessible places that you cannot get at with a glass brush, such as the handles of cups, jugs and so on. The most commonly used shape, and the cheapest, is a pointed one.

If you like you can use the pointed agate pencil to draw a simple design on a lightly polished gold rim. You will see this done, among other places, on genuine Chinese plates.

You can recognize all liquid gold by its dark brown, almost black, colour. The gold sheen does not appear until firing.

Never put gold on top of china paints without an intermediate firing. If you do they will run together and produce a mauve colour that you cannot get off. (The American gold is an exception.) An ordinary coat of gold can, on the other hand, be removed after firing by means of a special gold eraser for china painting. You use it like an ordinary rubber.

How Gold is Applied

As a first exercise it will be best to choose a very simple border. You could use for example one of those shown on pp. 104–105.

The china is first cleaned with cellulose thinner. (Be careful not to inhale this!) The areas to be laid with gold must not be touched, since the print of warm fingers can spoil the colour. The border pattern is drawn with pencil or All Stabilo.

A long pointed flower brush is recommended for smooth gold bands, which will be discussed later, and for the borders described here. The brush must always be softened before use with cellulose thinner and dried gently in a non-fluffy cloth. Shake the bottle of gold paint well, since gold is apt to precipitate. You might try standing the bottle upside down. If you have a glass

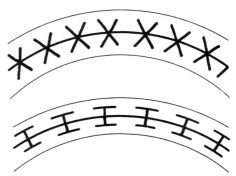

Patterns can be made from just a few lines.

spatula – a glass rod with a flat end – you can stir the contents of the bottle with it, and it can also be used for taking out the paint on to the mixing tile. If you have not got a glass spatula the gold can be taken out with the handle of the brush, as you did with oil. The gold is ready for use as soon as it comes out of the bottle. You should take only a few drops at a time, since it goes a long way; it will then stay liquid longer.

If the gold gets too thick you can add a few drops of gold thinner, but only a few drops – too much can give the gold a mauve tinge after firing. Similarly the use of a metal palette knife should be avoided, since it will darken or discolour the paint; gold can be mixed with a horn spatula if you have not got a glass one. Gold always gets more supple as it is mixed. You can also use oil of lavender for thinning, but again only in drops, since this thinning medium can give the coat a light red tinge if you use too much. Oil of lavender slows up the drying process.

By now both the gold and the brush are ready for use. Draw the point of the brush gently through the gold and paint up the drawn pattern with smooth, even strokes. Gold must be put on thick – how thick, you will learn to know by instinct as you work with it. But it can be hard to judge at first, as the gold dries nearly black. If in doubt there is no reason why you should not apply an extra coat when the first is quite dry. Gold applied too thin can disappear completely in the firing.

If you want a particularly durable coat of gold you can put on two coats with an intermediate firing, possibly using bright gold the first time and matt gold the second. If any gold is accidentally put on outside the pattern it must be cleaned off at once. You can do that with a little cotton wool moistened with water and rolled firmly on to the point of the brush handle. Naphtha can also be used. The slightest gold stain or suggestion of a print from a 'gold finger' on the white china will stand out conspicuously after firing. You must therefore be particularly careful about cleaning before the dry, hardened china is sent to be fired. Give it a final polish round the motif with cellulose thinner; you can also use gold thinner for this, but it becomes a bit expensive in the long run.

Silver

You can also work with silver, which is actually a mixture of fine gold with bright platinum. You work with it in the same way as with gold, but silver can prove a bit more awkward than gold in the firing, and you quite often have to give it an additional firing. It must be applied very smoothly and polished afterwards with a glass brush.

Cleaning

Clean the brushes and other materials used with cellulose thinner. If a brush stiffens after being used with gold it can be softened and cleaned with naphtha. Naphtha can also be used for thinning and has the advantage that it dries quickly, so that the gold does not spread so easily where it is not wanted.

Never use the same brushes for gold and for china paints, however well you clean them. A brush once used for paint will discolour the gold.

Patterns in Gold and Colour

When you have had some practice with simple gold borders you can go on to larger and more demanding tasks. But use gold with caution. China quickly becomes over-decorated with gold, and instead of an attractive result you get something that looks cheap and shoddy.

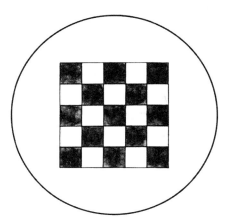

Chequered pattern for a glass tray in gold and blue ground.

Gold can be used in conjunction with colours (with an intermediate firing) and can be shaded with ordinary china paints, though the result is not always very effective. Gold is really a material that needs to stand by itself – after all, you would never dream of wearing costume jewelry with a gold bracelet. But if you treat the gold as it deserves, and the paint likewise, the combination can be very fine.

The chequered pattern illustrated above, quite simple and timeless, is intended for a glass or bottle tray. (For the drawing, see p. 103.)

The large square (in the circle) is drawn first with All Stabilo. You then lay a colour over the whole field in the form of a blue ground, which you can lay as you lay an ordinary ground. Use pale blue.

After an intermediate firing draw in the squares, then paint every other square with gold. Any kind of gold can be used. Then clean up round the motif, which is now finished and ready for firing.

For really special occasions you could also use a contrast between types of gold, laying bright gold in every other square and burnished gold in the others. Such a glass tray would be a splendid addition to a table service decorated only with a gold border. If you liked you could also add a simple gold border to the glass trays.

Putting on Smooth Gold Borders

It is almost impossible to put an absolutely smooth gold border on a round object freehand. For this purpose you need a banding wheel, which is a metal turntable on which the china is laid. The banding wheel is slowly rotated with the left hand while the right hand holds the brush with the gold absolutely still. For this use a brush with slanted hairs. Beginners can use a long, pointed flower brush for smooth borders, but a brush with slanted hairs is best.

To support your arm you use a wooden frame about 20cm. × 60cm. (8in. × 24in.), fitted to the table at shoulder height. Without these two tools (and a steady hand) you had better leave the painting of gold or coloured borders to the firing centre. If you do acquire the tools it will be as well to practise with coloured borders before going on to gold. Uneven borders can be corrected with a brush dipped in turpentine.

You need a little more oil in the paint than you use in an ordinary mixture.

It takes a lot of practice to learn to use a banding wheel, and not many private china painters own one.

Monograms

Monograms on china can look very smart, depending of course on how they are painted. If you want monograms in gold you should first find a beautiful and appropriate script. The letters should be simple and not too highly decorated, and the monogram not too big and striking. Draw the monogram and then apply two coats of gold. The work must be done very precisely and carefully – the least inaccuracy in a monogram will make it look clumsy. There are many good books of monograms which may prove helpful.

38. Relief Work in Gold

Relief Work on China

Early in the history of china ceramic artists tried to create sculptural forms in china – both as figures and as reliefs. Reliefs were often used as decorations on such things as jars and vases. Functional china is seldom done in relief today, and china is not in fact a very good material for relief work, since the effectiveness of a relief stems from the contrast of light and shade, and china does not provide the best conditions for that.

However, you will see unpainted china (especially German china) with panels in relief – presumably made especially for those who paint china as a hobby – but it is still debatable whether this form of decoration is really suited to china and whether there is really a case for painting such reliefs. Another form of relief is made when colours are put on in such a way as to give the effect of relief. But here too there is some doubt about the tastefulness of this procedure, whether or not you like the technique or think it appropriate to china. Many people say that the process is foreign to china.

A pattern can also be given a relief effect with gold.

Grinding

Draw the desired pattern on the china with the All Stabilo pencil, and for the gold relief grind the following with a horn spatula:

3mm. gold underlay
plus a third relief oil
plus turpentine for thinning

The gold underlay is a yellowish powder containing finely ground porcelain chips to which gold-coloured enamel is added. Add more turpentine if the paint does not flow. If necessary, add an extra drop of oil.

Drawing

Using a pointed flower brush draw the outline with the

paint. This must be done with precision. The stroke must remain tacky and half-glossy, and must not be liquid. It is best not to correct the stroke, since that easily makes the design uneven and causes it to lift in firing. If the brush will not run freely during the drawing, add another drop or two of relief oil. But do not put in too much or the stroke will run during firing.

An optical illusion. The white field on the bottom looks bigger than the black field on the top of the drawing.

Firing and Application of Gold
Dry the china well and send it for an intermediate firing. After the firing put on the gold in an even coat over the design and then send for firing again, this time at a temperature of not more than 1,380°F. (750°C.). Warn the firing centre about this. The result of this process is that the relief paint stands out as a raised, matt stroke in the gold.

Relief Paints
When relief effects are used the gold coat should not be polished too much. You can use bright gold if you prefer; this does not need polishing after application.

You can draw with pen and sugar paint as a basis for the gold, but you will obtain the best results if you use the real gold underlay. Gold can be applied to the relief paint without an intermediate firing, but it often gives a poor, dull look over the relief, and on balance intermediate firing is recommended. Never put on the gold underlay in broad areas, but always in thin lines, and do not put on too much. As you know, it is in his moderation that the master reveals himself.

List of suppliers

General UK Suppliers
Fulham Pottery Co., Ltd.,
210, New Kings Road,
Fulham,
London SW6 4NY.

Harrison Mayer Ltd.,
Meir,
Stoke-on-Trent,
Staffordshire.

Wengers Ltd.,
Etruria,
Stoke-on-Trent,
Staffordshire.

Podmore & Sons Ltd.,
New Caledonian Mills,
Shelton,
Stoke-on-Trent,
Staffordshire.

McNeal (cohn) Ltd.,
Meir,
Stoke-on-Trent,
Staffordshire.

US Suppliers
Brushes
M. Grumbacher, Inc.,
460 West 34th Street,
New York, N.Y. 10001.

Robert Simmons Inc.,
510, Sixth Avenue,
New York, N.Y. 10011.

A. Langnickel, Inc.,
115 West 31st Street,
New York, N.Y. 10001.

Yasutomo & Company,
24, California Street,
San Francisco,
California 94111.

Chinaware
Holbein Art Materials
23 Ueshiomachi 2-Chome,
Minami-ku,
Osaka, Japan.

Winsor & Newton Inc.,
555 Winsor Drive,
Secaucus,
New Jersey 07094
The Craftint
Manufacturing Co.,
18501 Eucild Avenue,
Cleveland, Ohio 44112.

Colours
The American Crayon
Company,
1706 Hayes Avenue,
Post Office Box No 2067,
Sandusky, Ohio 44870.

Steward Clay Company
113, Mulberry Street,
New York, N.Y. 10013

The T.H. Greenwood
Company,
Pennsylvania & Logan
Avenue,
North Hills, Pennsylvania.

Index